KEITH PETER WILSON

Just Lookin' Out of the Window

LIFE'S LESSONS FROM MY MOTHER

JUST LOOKIN' OUT OF THE WINDOW
Life's Lessons From My Mother

Keith Peter Wilson
aphikwdent@gmail.com

ISBN: 978-1-949027-76-1

Printed in the United States of America.
First printing edition 2021.

www.DestinedToPublish.com

TABLE OF CONTENTS

DEDICATION

This book is dedicated to God, who ordered these steps; my Father James, the rock that our household is built on; my Mother Alease, who was the heart and soul of my family; my sisters Ramona and Vanessa, the spirit of our family; and my wife Denise, the joy of my life.

Just lookin' out of the window

ACKNOWLEDGEMENTS

I have to first and foremost acknowledge the love of my life, my wife Denise Jackson-Wilson, who kept asking me to write a book for many years. She knew that writing was one of my passions, but I just wouldn't put the time into it. Denise made me believe that I had something to say that people might find interesting, so here it is! Thank you for the years of love and support as you held my heart in your hands!

Andrew Lyke, the Director of the Office of Black Catholics for the Archdiocese of Chicago, allowed me to write a column for the Drumline Newsletter and to talk about social issues of consequence in the Black Catholic community. This really had me wanting to write more. I hadn't written on a regular basis for years. I enjoyed my stint as a featured writer, and, when that ended, I missed writing for the public. Thank you for that column, my brother!

Ms. Marchel'le Renise Barber, the owner of Martha's Cribs Collectables and a former writer for Jet and Ebony magazines, edited my story and gave my voice clarity. She also did some research for this project that only a seasoned journalist could do, in addition to editing to ensure that historical items referenced were well-sourced and accurate. You made this book better!

Steven P. Smith, my fraternity brother and friend and the owner of Photographix Photography, knew my personality quirks and style of expression. He was one of my final sets of eyes during the efforts to establish the visual esthetic and physical presentation of the book, including my photo selection and the organization of the chapters. Thank you, brother.

I thank Cristal Simmons, the granddaughter of Bernice Kennedy Hendrix, a wonderful woman whom my dad fatefully met when they were both employees at the Morrison Hotel. This woman offered my dad the opportunity to rent an apartment in the building her family was purchasing, and the rest, as they say, is history! My friend Cristal filled in so many of the blanks regarding my parents' early married life for me. I thank you for that, my friend! Being that you love history, you truly personify Delta Sigma Theta Sorority. The Lambda Chapter that initiated you and your current chapter, Chicago Alumni, are lucky to have you!

My mom was my first cheerleader. She was very proud of my school projects and achievements. So, when I started to work unofficially with her to collect family stories about growing up in our old Chicago Southside neighborhood, this book became a labor of love. I realized that God had bestowed the gift of a great family upon me.

They say that God is love. My parents provided that to me and my sisters. This book aims to absolutely honor my mother and father, who provided the blueprint for my life. Exodus 20:12 speaks to this. It is also one of the 10 Commandments.

My dad is the commander-in-chief of the Wilson family. He chose my mother, who chose him back! This man has been through many wars as a Black man in this country and was the final person to approve the mission that is this book. His strength, along with my mother's love, is why my family was able to endure many storms. I love the man named James Taylor Wilson and thank him for teaching me how to be a man!

I am also thankful to have two wonderful sisters, Vanessa and Yvette. Like me, they have been constant students and admirers of our parents. I could not ask for better sisters, and I love you both! We are family! I got all my sisters and me!

I have had many great friends and confidants who have made my life better! I speak of many in this book, but a set of twins and their family in particular provided love, support, and joy during many of my important life adventures. We don't always get to spend time with each other, but my life is better because you have been in it. Thank you, my brothers from another mother!

Arnold Mireles, my other compadre from another madre, was my first friend! He showed me how to cook tortillas on a gas stove. He taught me about art. He played music on his record player for me. I remember that first day in a scary new school in the 3rd grade: he welcomed me into that school and into his life. I miss you dearly! Thank you for teaching me how to be a friend! Every friend since has had to measure up to you! Tell your mom and dad to check on my mom up in Heaven! I miss your mom's Christmas tortillas!

I have had some foes and even experienced some betrayal at the hands of people in my life circle. You also made my life what it is. For that, I thank you for teaching me painful but necessary life lessons. In life we have to take the good with the bad!

Marilyn Alexander, my publisher at Destined to Publish, put all of the final touches on this book and made my vision real. Thank you for making my first book look so good, my sister!

There are just too many others to name, including neighbors, aunts, uncles, cousins, coworkers, church mates, fraternity brothers, mentees, and other people who were in my life for a minute, a season, or a moment.

All I can say is thank you all for being part of my story!
Keith

Just lookin' out of the window

PREFACE

Where do dreams come from? I think they are grown in your soul, cultivated in your mind and seen with your eyes.

My earliest memories are when my family lived on the seventh floor of public housing on 26th and Prairie, in Chicago's Bronzeville community. I vividly remember when we moved from that seventh-floor apartment into our first home on Chicago's South Side. This modest home was a dream come true for my parents and life-changing for the whole family.

I was six years old at the time, and at that age, I really did not know that I was a dreamer. I simply took my cues from my mother, who helped guide me through life and offered me a perspective on how to view the world.

Most importantly, my mother wanted to show me her perspective on life that would help me and all in her family to do better. Being better does not mean seeing myself as better than other people. But she wanted us to learn that we should always be working and striving to DO better as people.

From the seventh-floor porch of our housing project, I could see my mom wearing her white lab jacket and scrubs, heading off each day to her job at Mercy Hospital, located just across the street. I could also see downtown Chicago with its fancy glass-encased buildings sitting on Lake Michigan just beyond that hospital.

Porches in the projects are very sterile, concrete platforms with chain link fencing preventing residents from falling to the ground below. Because of that metal wire, some who lived in these buildings also felt caged. When you grip those chain link fences as a kid, you can feel the limits of your world while attempting to visualize through them.

My two younger sisters and I shared that view from the porch when we stayed with Jane Milton, who lived down the hall from us. She was our neighbor, surrogate mother and babysitter who cared for us while our parents worked at their various jobs.

Our father was a real-life mailman who always came home each day and delivered safety, security and strength to us. He was the man coming through the doors in his blue uniform to see his family!

Mom was the soul and hope of our family. She was the ring leader of our little circus and kept us on track! Always forward! Better! Brighter! Move! She was the dreamer!

Our parents gave us kids real balance. Dad was stern, while Mom was sweet. Dad could seem impatient, while Mom could seem like time had no meaning. They were a "yin and yang" couple. But at the end of the day, *they* were our world, and we were theirs.

Music playing and festive family meals were the rule at our home. Whether it was fried bologna or grilled cheese on white bread, you appreciated what you had, even while dreaming of something better. For my parents, "something better" was a home in another South Side neighborhood of Chicago, about 15 miles away.

Everywhere my parents lived would eventually lead to a place our family could call home. If we had lived in a barn, my parents would have transformed it into a comfortable dwelling. Indeed, an address does not determine the outcome of your life or the final destination of the people living there. My mom always said that we might not have a lot of money, but we were not poor. Being poor, she insisted, was an attitude.

While growing up, I didn't know that I was a part of something special, but as I got older, I began to see that I was blessed. I have a father who was always present and available and a mother married to a man she loved. Together, their priority was doing what was best for their children. When my parents made a promise, it was as reliable as the sun rising and setting. They never let us down!

Maybe that is why I love to look at the sky and the sun. I also love to see the waters of Lake Michigan. Its water is so calming, I could look at it every day. When I am a little down, all I have to do is close my eyes and think about my parents and my wife, Denise, who have brought that kind of joy to my life.

When I close my eyes and think about my family, I hear music. My dad was the music director with a baritone voice who taught the family the main verses, which stressed protecting your family and making them first in your life! Mom, the co-music director, taught us the chorus, which was about having faith in both good and bad times. Both would teach their three children the melody, which stressed the importance of always getting along with your neighbor and understanding how to stay grounded.

Mom would occasionally take me, her oldest offspring, off to the side and make me go through my scales. Her private lessons were necessary in case she would one day need her firstborn to use the bass in his voice to lead a song and direct a family of his own.

Mom was ever the dreamer, because she saw things in her family and the people around her that only someone who believes in God could see. "If you have that house built on the firm foundation of family and faith, you can't lose," my mother would always say.

Our seventh-floor apartment also had windows with unique views of the City of Chicago and Lake Michigan. Glass windows have the unique trait of being clear and allowing views from both sides. From the inside of a window, you can see the outside world, and conversely, the outside world can see in.

Glass can shield and protect us from the elements of the outside world, but at the same time, it can't provide protection from any hard projectiles pushed in from the outside during a storm. As the singer says, "storms will come, this we know for sure!"

There are also times when that very clear glass can paradoxically hide impending danger. One time when I was with my dad, visiting one of his co-workers who lived in one of the rowhouses in the Cabrini–Green housing projects, I walked straight through their glass sliding door. I had never used a sliding door and didn't see the glass!

At five or six years old, I really didn't understand how glass worked, but I learned the hard way on that day. That was one of many life lessons I would learn: things are not always what they seem!

When you are growing up, the smallest things can have such an impact on how you see the world. It is also in those small things that dreams can hide. I think learning to dream makes you always want to move forward to something better.

At times, dreams can also come at a cost that you have to pay. Sometimes dreams are pleasant, while others are nightmares! I continue to dream. I think I learned about dreaming the most from my mother.

When my parents moved us out of those projects into their dream house on the South Side, I was entering the first grade with three simple dreams: a brother, a dog and a piano. Some of those dreams didn't come true until I was much older, while others never came true at all.

But I thank God for those simple dreams! In time, I learned to keep remembering my dreams and sometimes to just take a minute to notice what is right outside of my window.

Newlyweds Alease and James Wilson September 1958 in Chicago

Just lookin' out of the window

CHAPTER 1
Just Lookin' Out of the Window

My name is Keith P. Wilson, and I was born on May 15, 1963, in Chicago, Illinois. This book is a series of my recollections and memories about growing up on the South Side of Chicago in the years after my family left Chicago public housing and purchased their first home to start a new chapter with their three children.

I found many parallels in my life with another family that also came from the projects of Chicago: the fictional Evans family on the iconic television show *Good Times*.

Good Times premiered with an episode called "Too Old Blues" on February 8, 1974. The pilot episode was centered around James Evans, who had just applied to participate in a union apprenticeship program that would help him earn more money to support his family. James is disappointed when he is told that he is too old to join the union, and the episode explores his disappointment.

Creators Eric Monte and Mike Evans and Executive Producer Norman Lear worked together to create a show reflecting Black life in urban Chicago, which was revolutionary at the time. The show would become one of the most iconic television shows in American broadcasting history.

Good Times was instrumental in introducing the realities of African-American life to the general public. Laced with comedy and tragedy,

Good Times premiered on the CBS network and broadened awareness of African-American culture throughout the world.

The "Too Old Blues" pilot episode, like later *Good Times* episodes, focused on the challenges faced by the Evans family. The five-member family experienced continual poverty, racism, poor health care, crime and a lack of opportunity to advance their condition.

The backdrop for *Good Times* demonstrated to America the many challenges faced by people who live in government-subsidized housing, also known as the "projects." From rats and cockroaches scampering about the tall industrial-style buildings to intimidating hoodlums who sometimes terrorized the residents inside, *Good Times* made it clear that people who had few other options lived in public housing.

The central theme of each *Good Times* episode was that it would use comedy while showing the serious realities and challenges of black urban life. Viewers would learn of the Evans family's struggles while following their attempts to leave the projects and move on to a better life.

In many of the episodes, the Evans family members or other memorable characters on were set up to see opportunity within their reach but often had their dreams shattered. But there was beauty and strength in their struggles!

Good Times as a television series was similar to the popular blaxploitation movies that were the rage in movie theaters during the 1970s. Roots, a 1977 television miniseries written by Alex Haley, would later secure much of the *Good Times* audience. The comedy-based *Good Times* likely helped to prepare the country for a national discussion on race as a new televised experience involving the brutal history of chattel slavery in the U.S. when the epic and historic Roots miniseries aired a few years later.

I was in the fifth grade when the historic Roots broadcasts were taking place. In many ways, these diverse 1970s television shows illustrated how African-American viewers can laugh at our lives while watching *Good Times*, but also experience visceral anger when viewing

2

the brutality of slavery portrayed in Roots. We as a Black people often need to laugh in order not to cry!

Prior to the debut of *Good Times*, Chicago was experimenting with youth-oriented television programing and shows that could attract Black audiences. Don Cornelius, a Black back-up disc jockey at WVON radio, was hired by the television station WCIU in 1967. He worked at the station in various broadcasting capacities while also producing Chicago-area "record hops" at high schools to promote the television station. Soon, Cornelius's community caravan events were famously dubbed the "Soul Train."

Sears, Roebuck & Company, also based in Chicago, became sponsors of *Soul Train*, which premiered on WCIU-TV on August 17, 1970, in a weekly live show format. *Soul Train* would feature mostly African-American entertainers while also capturing the attention of music lovers of all races and ages.

Most of the entertainers who performed on *Soul Train* were "lip syncing" to recordings of their most popular hits in front of cameras while the program's dancers moved to the beat. Some of the most famous entertainers on the *Soul Train* stage were the Jackson 5, James Brown, Marvin Gaye, Stevie Wonder, B.B. King and Diana Ross.

African-Americans loved the dances they saw performed on the show and would attempt to recreate them during family reunions or events where large numbers of people were in attendance. The most famous event seen on Soul Train was the very popular "Soul Train Line." Created using the show's largely unpaid dancers, the Soul Train Line was actually similar to the 1950s dance fad known as "The Stroll." The Soul Train Line would begin when the dancers formed two long lines with a wide space in the middle so selected dancers could come forward and strut their stuff down the line and in front of *Soul Train's* cameras.

Once *Soul Train* became nationally syndicated, the dance was updated, often using professional dancers and people who used the national spotlight to open doors to careers in entertainment for themselves. The group Shalamar actually was a byproduct of Mr.

Cornelius being wowed by the "Pop Locking" of *Soul Train* dancer Jeffrey Daniel, who was a founding member of the group.

Soul Train was also known for its groundbreaking commercials, which promoted products created and sold by Black businesses. One of Soul Train's largest advertising accounts was with George E. Johnson, the Founder and President of the Black-owned Johnson Products Company based in Chicago.

These now-celebrated commercials featured Black actors and actresses who promoted products aimed at the Black consumer. Afro Sheen and Ultra Sheen commercials were very popular because these trendy products made to target the Black hair-care market also mingled a taste of Black culture and pride into the hour-long nationally televised shows.

One memorable Afro Sheen commercial on *Soul Train* featured a Black actor portraying Frederick Douglass. This historical character was one of America's most famous escaped slaves, who became an abolitionist and newspaper publisher.

In the commercial, Douglass speaks to a younger Black male character who, in his opinion, has poorly maintained hair. Douglass looks at the young man's hairstyle with disapproval, and the young man responds by saying, "Well, Mr. Douglass, you know times have changed. We wear the Natural now." Douglass responds with the funniest line in the commercial: "You call that a Natural?" Keep in mind, Douglass had one of the wildest Afros in history, which makes the banter hilarious!

Indeed, for many, the most memorable part of watching *Soul Train* was studying these commercials. Blacks who wanted to see what we needed to purchase for our hair and skin and how to wear the latest styles just needed to watch an hour of *Soul Train!*

Soul Train took the show to a national audience after relocating the show to Los Angeles. It soon became clear that while the show was selling Black entertainment and ethnic products aimed primarily at Blacks, *Soul Train* was also selling Black pride to America. The show became syndicated in 1971 and ran nationally until 2006.

As a result of *Soul Train*, Black music was becoming more popular in America and around the world. *Soul Train*, while promoting mostly R&B-style music, soon rivaled Dick Clark's American Bandstand, which had a primarily White audience with a pop music format. As I watched *Good Times* and *Soul Train*, I observed that both television shows seemed to make Whites more comfortable with seeing African-Americans on their television screens.

It was still a treat for people to see the rainbow of colors being added to network television. Both *Good Times* and *Soul Train* took the scary edge off of urban Blacks who often were portrayed on television as criminals or domestics.

In the '70s, many Whites didn't have a full understanding of the Civil Rights Movement. The rise of the Nation of Islam frightened them even more, as many Whites were fearful of both Blacks and the Islamic faith. Unfortunately, some Whites still have these same fears even though it is now 2021!

Good Times would be one of a number of successful Black-themed television shows produced by Norman Lear. Among them was the sitcom *Sanford and Son*, televised on the NBC network from 1972 through 1977. The show was led by comedian Redd Foxx, who portrayed a junk dealer. He had a live-in adult son, Lamont Sanford, portrayed by Demond Wilson. The father-and-son junk dealers often disagreed about how to run the business, which was the essence of both the comedy and the tension between the two main characters.

I watched this show and laughed at its edgy comedy. *Sanford and Son* was another show about Black urban life that seemed to make Whites feel comfortable about a growing and more influential Black population by exposing them to a non-threatening vicarious urban experience. Chicagoan Quincy Jones penned the memorable theme song called "The Streetbeater."

Often, Norman Lear would take actresses or actors from one of his shows and use their talents to help develop completely different television shows. Lear found the matron of his future hit television show *Good Times*, Esther Rolle, after she played the maid Florida in another of his shows *Maude*, itself a spin-off from *All in the Family*. Chicago soul singer Donny Hathaway composed and sang the theme song for *Maude*, giving that show some Chicago soul during its opening and closing credits.

Mr. Hathaway was one of a number of Chicago soul singers, including Curtis Mayfield, who were big musical influences at that time. Hathaway received his musical training at the storied music program of Howard University in Washington, D.C., where he also was initiated into Alpha Phi Alpha Fraternity. Mr. Hathaway and a female Chicago postal worker named Nadine McKinnor would eventually write a Black Christmas anthem titled "This Christmas." My family played that 45 record every Christmas after its release in 1971. Donny Hathaway also would team up with fellow crooner Roberta Flack in many memorable duets that would capture the essence of the times. "Where is the Love?"

When Esther Rolle was cast as the Evans family matron Florida, she changed the course of television history. Rolle had a contractual requirement that her character Florida be a married woman. As an established actress in her own right, Rolle refused to participate in a television show that offered negative stereotypes of Black families and lacked a Black father figure. This was a major principled stand that she took against the producers of the show, who wanted her to be a single mother in the role.

John Amos was cast in the role of husband James Evans, though he was actually nineteen years younger than Rolle. This critical element of a present male figure in the household is another reason the show made television history by shattering negative stereotypes of African-American life!

In a similar fashion, Diahann Carroll's character Julia, a widowed single mother and nurse, had previously introduced the concept of a Black professional woman to the American psyche when her show *Julia* premiered in 1968. This show, which ran on NBC until 1971, was groundbreaking because it was the first weekly series to star an African-American woman in a non-stereotypical role, as opposed to our usual role as servants. Sponsors were very sensitive to the implications of race relations and were always trying to err on the side of not offending White audiences.

Another pivotal TV moment for Blacks on television occurred on November 22, 1968, when the first televised interracial kiss took place on Star Trek between Nichelle Nichols (Lt. Nyota Uhura), a Black woman, and William Shatner (Captain James T. Kirk), a White man. Another, more lighthearted interracial kiss was when Sammy Davis Jr. kissed Archie Bunker on the cheek on an episode of *All in the Family*.

Times and sensibilities about race were changing, albeit slowly, but the popularity of shows with predominately Black casts on television suggests that views were slowly changing for the better.

The Uhura character on Star Trek was itself groundbreaking as the first Black female portrayed in a position of leadership. She was in a command position as a lieutenant serving on the bridge of the fictional Starship Enterprise. A little Black girl from Chicago named Mae Jemison would be inspired to become an astronaut after seeing someone who looked like her on TV. Ms. Nichols became a real recruiter for NASA in the 1980s.

Nichols's role on *Star Trek* was seen as so critical that when she wanted to quit the series, she was implored by Rev. Dr. Martin Luther King Jr. to continue on the show because of the vital imagery she presented on television. Nichols also has Chicago ties, as she grew up in Robbins, a south suburb of Chicago. Positive Black imagery on TV was important to the famous and regular citizen alike.

When those shows are compared to today's shows, we see that television has certainly changed. Today's television has expanded to include cable networks that some say have created a sensational "anything goes" television experience. A kiss shared by a fictional interracial couple in 1968 that almost caused the cancelation of the show is very tame compared to the nudity and obscene language broadcast on television today.

Taking a stand and enforcing values helped propel television forward and often occurred *because* of African-American entertainers being cast in these roles and demanding these values. Rolle's demand to

7

have a father figure on *Good Times* was indeed an important paradigm shift in the portrayal of Blacks on TV, which also impacted the view that the population would have of our race. If Mr. Lear hadn't agreed to Rolle's terms, what would this first Black family of the modern television era have looked like? It is likely Rolle would have been seen as another Black stereotype on an "urban" show.

It was during this time frame that *Good Times* would blast onto the scene and into living rooms all across America. The soulful voice of Sondra " Blinky" Williams, with a familiar gospel cadence, would implore viewers in the catchy opening theme song to query, "Ain't we lucky we got 'em?" as a reference to life's "Good Times." Americans of all colors saw an African-American family, while at my home, I saw *my* family.

My family, like the Evans family at the end of the television series, would move on to a better neighborhood and a brighter future after leaving public housing in 1969. The genius of the TV series was the fateful teaming of two African-American men, Eric Monte and Mike Evans, the show's creators, with Jewish producer Norman Lear. The group would end up producing a show that allowed White America to get a glimpse of a small part of the soul of Black America in the '70s.

Eric Monte had already achieved notoriety for writing the movie *Cooley High*, another Chicago-based classic. Monte wrote the script of that movie based on the real Cooley High School located in Chicago near the Cabrini–Green housing projects. Chicago in the 1970s was an important landscape for the depiction of urban living in cities across the nation. *Cooley High* and *Good Times* both could have been set in Harlem, Detroit or the Watts neighborhood of Los Angeles. The names of the cities are different, but the African-American experiences in those urban centers are essentially the same. Monte is also the creator of the TV show *What's Happening*, an indirect spin-off of *Cooley High*.

Much has been made about the eventual buffoonery of the James Evans Jr. (J.J.) character in *Good Times*. Many African-Americans felt that the character had simply become foolish. Decades later, Black historians and social scientists are still debating this view in some aspects, but J.J.'s character continued to be a catalyst for storylines that forever will make the ensemble cast a generally decent representation of an African-American family.

An honest assessment of stereotypes does reveal that there is a certain degree of reality in every stereotype, but during the height of the popularity of shows aimed at Black audiences, many Civil Rights organizations panned *Good Times* and other Black shows for stereotypical images of African-Americans. There were similar complaints from the NAACP about blaxploitation movies, which also were the rage in the 1970s. The Black Panther Party under Huey Newton lodged complaints about Lear's portrayal of African-Americans in his shows.

Good Times promoted a very important, but underreported aspect of Black life in the '70s known as the "nuclear family." The stereotype of the absent Black father in the Black community was shattered by this show's portrayal of James Evans, who loved, respected and supported his family despite the challenges he faced. He was just like my dad!

As the family's head, James Evans Sr. projected a powerful image of the strong Black provider for his family. He was not an add-on or occasional bed buddy to Florida. He was a leader and partner in a loving marriage. James Evans Sr. would also stand up for each member of his family if he felt they were in danger. Residents of public housing were presented as multidimensional and not just "ghetto" dwellers.

The three Evans children were portrayed by versatile actors Jimmie Walker (James Evans Jr, a.k.a. J.J.), Bern Nadette Stanis (Thelma) and Ralph Carter (Michael). The latter two performers are actually natives of New York City, which probably gave them the needed urban sensibilities for their roles. Both were also accomplished singers and dancers. Ralph Carter had performed on Broadway in *Raisin* which was based on *A Raisin in The Sun* by Lorraine Hansberry. Stanis, who played the intelligent and beautiful Black teen Thelma, was very familiar with living in public housing because she lived in some as a youth. Jimmie Walker had also performed in *Let's Do It Again*, a popular blaxploitation movie with fellow *Good Times* costar John Amos.

Americans of all colors and backgrounds became very familiar with all of the members of the Evans family. The names of Florida, James, Thelma, J.J. and Michael Evans would forever be known as members of the Evans family on *Good Times*.

In every Black neighborhood, there was the "nosy neighbor," usually a lady who knew all the goings-on of the block or a floor in the "jets." This woman could usually be seen holding look-outs on the stoop of a walk-up or sitting in the chair on the porch outside of her apartment. Sometimes, the look-out spot was in the comfort of her living room in a row house, where the neighborhood was the picture for the window. The nosy neighbor on this show, the sassy Willona Woods, was played by Ja'Net DuBois. Willona was known as "the Rona Barrett of the ghetto," after a very popular White gossip columnist of the 1970s. In some ways, Jane Milton, our neighbor and babysitter on the seventh floor of our housing project, mirrored the Willona character. Mrs. Milton would become more like a family member than a babysitter who lived down the hall.

A number of other supporting characters on *Good Times* would also impact this family's story. A well-known character actress named Helen Martin portrayed "Weeping Wanda," another neighbor in the Evans family's project building. Helen Martin would provide comic relief in her portrayal of her character. Her physical features would always remind me of Jane Milton. Helen Martin would go on to become another similar nosey neighbor as Pearl Shay on another television show called 227. Her character would literally hang out on the front stoop of an apartment building in Washington, D.C. This show was created by Chicagoan Christine Houston and would star another daughter from the "City of Big Shoulders," Marla Gibbs. Marla Gibbs is a well-known character actress and a graduate of the famed Wendell Phillips High School located in Chicago's Bronzeville community. The housing project my family lived in was located near Wendell Phillips. Marla Gibbs would become the star of another Norman Lear creation, *The Jeffersons*, as Florence the maid.

One constant theme throughout *Good Times* was that the Evans family desired to better their station in life. For the Evans family, living in public housing was meant to be only a stepping stone, not a place where they planned to live for the rest of their lives. Just like my parents.

The constant effort each individual Evans family member or neighboring character made to better their station highlighted how each person was working on ways to try and better themselves and their family. The "American 'can do' spirit" made this story relatable to its loyal viewers, regardless of race or class.

Introducing *Good Times* are the words and music that create a jovial message of struggle. The words "Keeping your head above water" let viewers know that the Evans family will most likely experience this constant struggle in each episode of the show. Who can't relate to the life drama of taking one step forward, then later being forced to take three steps backwards?

The Evans family was like many families I remember when my family lived in public housing. My parents were like most residents of public housing in that their jobs didn't pay well, so they had multiple jobs to make ends meet. The media would also have you believe that there were no fathers in the projects, but there were many fathers living in public housing with their families. My parents had an end apartment on the seventh floor of a building at 2611 S. Prairie Avenue, apartment #708 in the Bronzeville community.

In order to make ends meet, Dad had two jobs. One was at the Main Chicago Post Office as a mail sorter, and he had a second job as a laborer at the headquarters of the Montgomery Ward (Wards). His job at Wards was literally blocks from the Cabrini–Green housing complex portrayed on *Good Times*. Two of the biggest retailers in the world, Sears and Montgomery Ward, were both founded in Chicago and were well known for their catalogues. While my father worked his two jobs, my mother made her contribution to the family budget by working at Mercy Hospital, which was located across the street from our complex.

Good Times showed the world that Black people who lived in public housing were also hard working and family-oriented people. I knew this fictional family on television because it was my family!

During our time living in public housing, I observed people who wanted better for themselves and their families. Public housing was more than a trope of places where crime was the rule of the day and single mothers were raising bad kids.

People of all races and classes often negatively stereotype the people who live in public housing. In the minds of many, these unattractive industrial-style buildings represent urban blight where lazy and unmotivated people live. But in real life, many people would eventually rise from these concrete cages and become very successful citizens. While there were also stories of failure and crime, they were the exception.

It is important to note that public housing from its inception had the mission of being transitional housing. The Robert Taylor Homes housing projects were another set of projects in Chicago and probably the second most infamous in the city, with a reputation that rivaled Cabrini–Green. They were named after the first African American Chairman of the Chicago Housing Authority.

The Cabrini–Green projects were among the largest in the nation when they were built in 1942. Things that went on in those buildings became infamous in Chicago lore. Our real building at 2611 S. Prairie was near other projects including the Ickes, the Hilliard Homes, Robert Taylor and the Ida B. Wells Housing Projects.

One thing that anyone who has actually lived in public housing understands is that life there is often about trying to make it to the next day. Today is always an adventure, while hoping the janitor will finally come fix the sink or spray the roaches, and tomorrow is an unknown.

"WHERE IS BUFFALO BUTT WHEN YOU NEED HIM?"

SEP • 68 •

Picture of me on my bike with my younger sister Vanessa Lynn 2611 S Prairie, Apt #708 Bronzeville, Chicago September 1968, Age 5

Just lookin' out of the window

CHAPTER 2
View From My Mother's Window

A couple of years ago, I rekindled the habit of writing my thoughts on a daily basis. I used to journal every day as a young person, capturing the events in my little notebook that I kept. I started journaling when I was eight years old in 1971, after transferring to a new Catholic school in the third grade. This new school was a very nurturing environment and a sanctuary compared to the neighborhood public school I transferred from. I never told anyone about my secret Meade spiral notebook into which I would write my thoughts.

My mother was instrumental in this move to Catholic school. This change impacted my life in every aspect. Attending Catholic school and the Catholic faith changed my life forever! That decision my parents made to invest money that they really didn't have in the education of me and my siblings has paid a lifetime of dividends for me.

Catholic school is where I discovered my love for music, science, public speaking and writing. Catholic education has its foundation in a faith that has taken me years to understand and develop. My mother wanted her children to understand that what you are today is not what you have to be tomorrow.

"Always try to do better" was my mother's mantra. She stressed that people are actors who may act really smart or strong, but are actually neither. Just because you don't have a lot today doesn't mean that you will be in that same situation tomorrow, according to her.

As I got older, I didn't write as often, but I would occasionally throw a thought or two down on some random pieces of paper. In 2017, I had a lot of new free time when some friends of mine and I decided to protest the treatment of Colin Kaepernick by boycotting watching football on television. I decided to use this free time to start writing again. For years I had been trying to write a book, but I always would get distracted or too busy. I used those months with the TV off to do something different by putting my words into book form.

I began to write in earnest each Sunday when I was not watching the game. I also started listening to some of my favorite music again. I started playing my favorite groups and picked up my old hobby of DJing. I made sure to play my many Earth, Wind & Fire records. This music inspired me and took me back to a fun time in my life in the 1970s.

A friend of mine named Tracey Love started an old-school radio show on Facebook, and I became very inspired by much of the music that he played. I really enjoyed listening to the music of my youth on my turntable in my home with the occasional hissing and popping needle on the rotating vinyl. Listening to that music helped me relieve the stressors of 20-plus years as a general dentist.

My parents are both really great storytellers. Myself and my two sisters, Vanessa and Ramona, learned about life growing up in the South by listening to their stories. My parents would talk about what it was like when they and other Blacks first migrated to Chicago from their hometown of Nashville, Tennessee. Listening to their stories fostered my interest in history and storytelling.

Starting in 2015, I found myself spending a lot more time with my parents, especially after the death of my mother-in-law, Juanita Jackson, in September of that year. Her death reminded me that I had a finite amount of time to spend with my own parents. My parents had been married for 58 years in 2015, and we were doing a lot of reminiscing as my sisters and I were planning for their upcoming 60th wedding anniversary celebration in 2017. Going through old family photos and videos really took me back to those wonderful years of my youth.

My grandmother Otie B. Smith turned 100 in June 2015, and my sisters and I also coordinated a reunion/celebration around that milestone in Nashville. Though she was Dad's mother, there were people from my mother's family also present at the celebration. My parents grew up a couple of blocks from each other and both families know each other, which made the event an opportunity to reconnect with both sides of my heritage. Being around so many family members and friends was touching. I reconnected with my extended Wilson and Owens family members that I had become disconnected from years ago. That family celebration brought us back together again.

My mother always told me to remember family. Family was important to her, and I internalized that message. I was very close to my immediate family, but not so much to many of my cousins, aunts and uncles back in Nashville, because I didn't visit very much as an adult. As a result, I started a family Facebook page in 2015 to get reconnected with my extended family.

Between 2015 and 2017, I drove my parents back to Nashville a number of times to visit relatives back in Tennessee, often unfortunately to attend the funerals of their aging siblings. While I was sitting in the driver's seat going down Interstate 65 with my senior parents as passengers, those drives brought back memories of many family trips to Nashville. During those trips, my mom and dad served as pilot and co-pilot. A big difference now was that I could say "I am the captain now!" during those trips. I was now doing the driving and also feeding my parents during those trips, just like they once did for my sisters and me during the family's annual trips to Nashville. I love my parents, and it was an honor to be in a position to say, "I got this, Mom and Dad!" It was during these trips and family time that I began to realize how much these two had done for me in my life.

I wanted to memorialize my wonderful memories of these trips while they were fresh in my mind, so I started writing down some of the memories of my youth. I also began to ask Mom and Dad about their memories of the exploits of my youth. I wanted to honor my mother and father as I had been taught long ago. Mom was my main collaborator for this project. When my family got together on Sundays, both parents helped me fill in details that I didn't always have right. Looking back, it seems like I was being directed by someone "above me" to write this story as a tribute to these two great parents.

One morning, I remember looking in the mirror at this guy who looked a bit different. This fellow was developing a receding hairline, had put on some weight and had aged a bit. I began to ponder the life of "The Man in the Mirror." I began to think about the many stories my parents shared about their lives growing up, and these memories made me think about my own life.

Both of my parents are gifted storytellers with comedic skills as well as a flair for the dramatic when telling a story. My mother can't tell one of her more humorous stories without bursting into spontaneous laughter. With her fantastic ability to recall the smallest details, she can take a story to another level.

When Dad tells a story, it is usually about a serious life event, but his stories are still humorous. I think Dad's use of humor in his stories was to mask the hurt he experienced in the midst of his pain growing up in Nashville. Mom's style was about finding good even in the midst of a really bad situation. Both of my parents are extremely strong people who know how to navigate hell with no water and come out on the other side. That is kind of a metaphor for life I learned from my parents.

I am so happy that I have a very close family that produced so many wonderful memories. I have always enjoyed our family dinners filled with lively conversations and laughter. The more family at these celebrations, the better.

As I began to write again, I remembered the family vacations, times in church or just family time gathered around the single household television. On that TV, we watched shows like *The Carol Burnett Show, Hee Haw and The Flip Wilson Show.* Dad loved his old Western movies, while Mom loved her gospel shows.

We kids loved watching cartoons on Saturday mornings. We viewed shows designed for children like *Romper Room and Ray Rayner* on weekday mornings before school. I am truly a child of the 1970s, which is when these shows were in their heyday. Many of the shows we watched regularly premiered in that decade.

Norman Lear began to produce some of the more serious and topical shows that we watched. His shows were groundbreaking, with many complicated themes. We also watched the old family shows of the 1960s, exemplified by *The Andy Griffith Show* and *The Dick Van Dyke Show*. Those shows were so popular that they are still aired today in reruns.

My parents were never afraid to talk about politics, religion or race, so I loved when Norman Lear put more edgy and topical shows like *All in the Family* and *Maude* on television. By 1973, I was a 10-year-old kid who routinely read the local newspaper for fun and loved those grown-up shows.

As I thought about how to tie in all of the adventures and exploits that have brought me through 58 years of life, I found parallels in the television show Good Times. That show represented the struggle of a family, their interactions with the world and the friends they chose.

My parents taught me that you can't choose your family, but you can choose your friends. The friends you choose reflect who YOU are. As I started writing, I began to remember various relationships that I had with girlfriends, old co-workers, people from church and even my ex-wife. I thought about how different relationships with people have made me into the person I am today.

There are some friends that I still see regularly, but on the other hand, I have not seen many of my friends for years. There are also people from my past that I will likely never see again. Whether I included your name and our exploits in this book or not, I thank you for making my life better, even if some hurt was involved.

My parents taught me to take people as they are. Mom taught me to be willing to forgive everyone for EVERYTHING, which requires true strength. But that does not mean I ever forget a hurt or a lie at the hands of another person, as that would be foolish!

Mom always said that YOU may want and need forgiveness from someone and never receive it, so forgive always, because forgiveness is really for you, not the other person. I have not been so good at that at times. While looking over my life, there have been people that I have avoided people because they either hurt me or that I have hurt. For that, I ask each of YOU to forgive me, because I have long ago forgiven YOU. I don't plan to leave this place anytime soon, but whenever my end occurs, I truly want to leave my story without any guilt.

I also wrote this book because I wanted to let certain people know how important they had been to me, but unfortunately, I waited too long and never got to tell them what was in my heart before they died, and for that I have some regrets.

I gave my mother a draft of this book on Mother's Day of 2019, three days before my 56th birthday. I have rewritten this book many times over these four years because I wanted it to be perfect. One of the lessons I learned from my mother is that there is no such thing as perfect, so I just prayed that she would just think it was good!

This is for you, Mom!

"JUST LOOKING THROUGH THE WINDOW."

CHAPTER 3
"The End of the Rainbow"

Good Times final series episode, originally aired August 1, 1979

As I look back over my family's story, I purposely chose the last episode of *Good Times* titled "The End of The Rainbow" as a parallel to the beginning of my family's story. In 1969, when my family made the life-changing move out of public housing into our first home, I was beginning first grade. At six years old, I was old enough to vividly recall life events that year, like the premiere of *Sesame* Street. That PBS show was so important to families with young children at that time. My parents essentially thought it was required viewing.

In those years, television included the three networks of ABC, CBS and NBC. Major cities had a local PBS affiliate like WTTW Channel 11 in Chicago. Big cities often also had Ultra High Frequency (UHF) channels, like channels 26, 32 and 44 in Chicago. The decade from 1969 to 1979 (when *Good Times* ended) were some of the most important years in my life. 1969 was the year that our family saw our rainbow and secured the pot of gold at the end of it.

Reaching the end of that proverbial rainbow is the point in a story where dreams are achieved and you finally can hold those hard-sought riches in your hands. But what is really at the end of that rainbow?

When I think about those years immediately after we moved out of public housing, it helps me understand my present and my future. Recounting the journey that my parents took us on helps me understand my life so much better. I have just started to understand that this path we tread is often the "stony road" necessary to strengthen us for life.

21

We, like the Evans family at the end of the series, moved on to a better neighborhood for a brighter and far more hopeful future. My parents had rented a number of apartments since their arrival in Chicago, but purchasing a home would be a fulfillment of their "American Dream."

The fictional Evans couple of James and Florida Evans had migrated northward from Mississippi as a part of the Great Migration. Based on the show's mid-1970s timeline and the age of the Evans children, you could estimate that the couple would have arrived in Chicago in the mid-1950s, during the second wave of the Great Northern Migration, which occurred from the 1940s to 1970. My parents, James and Alease Wilson, were real participants in that second wave when they relocated to Chicago from Nashville, Tennessee, between 1957 and 1958.

My parents married in Nashville, Tennessee, on August 8, 1957, in a civil service witnessed by my dad's cousin Robert "Sonny" Westmoreland. The wedding occurred at the courthouse in downtown Nashville. Both of my parents were 21 years old. They married six months after my dad completed his GED when he returned from the Marines. He had left high school in his junior year and served in the Marines for three years.

On their wedding day, Mom, Dad and Sonny rode public transportation to and from the simple ceremony. After the ceremony, mom went back to her mother Roberta Owens's home. The next day, Dad and Sonny took a train north to Chicago to prepare for a new life, but Dad's new bride would stay behind in Nashville for a few months until he found steady work. My father eventually took a job at the Morrison Hotel, and my parents finally settled together in Chicago in 1958.

The first neighborhood they moved into was located at 6441-43 South Ellis in the Woodlawn community near the University of Chicago. It was a one-room walkup that my mother hated! They eventually moved into an apartment in the Englewood community. Englewood would become one of a number of terminal destinations on the South Side of Chicago that many Blacks from southern states moved into after coming to Chicago.

Blacks during the Great Migration often moved north to cities like New York, Chicago and St. Louis looking for work. Neither of my parents had any education beyond high school, just like the fictional Evans couple on *Good Times*. My father, the hard-working James T. Wilson, could never be accused of being lazy, as he always worked multiple jobs to make ends meet, just like James Evans on our television. Like the Evans family, my parents didn't have much money, but they knew how to "make a dollar out of 15 cents."

My dad and his cousin Sonny grew up a couple doors from each other in Nashville. Both men attended Pearl High School together, though Sonny was one year older. They were just like brothers when they were growing up, though my father had five real brothers and three sisters, and Sonny also had siblings of his own. The cousins were thick as thieves in their youth. They worked many jobs together, including a job at a bowling alley on the White side of Nashville.

My father and his cousin would cut through Centennial Park late at night after their shift ended to get home. This was very dangerous because Blacks weren't allowed in the park after sunset, but this shortcut saved them time and money to get home. They could have caught a bus to get home, but the bus ride, in addition to costing money, also would have taken them out of the way through downtown. If they were caught in that park at night by any Whites, they would likely be beaten up. They also risked being harassed by White police officers who patrolled the park. The largest replica in the world of the Greek Parthenon is located in that same park. Imagine how much land they had to cross to get from one end to the other!

At age 17, my father decided that he wanted to join the Marines with Sonny. Because Dad was 17, his mother needed to sign for him so he could enlist. His mother, Otie B. Smith, wasn't really convinced that her son at 17 really knew what he was getting himself into, but after much convincing from the recruiter, she signed the paperwork so my dad could join the Marines with his cousin.

Grandma Otie, as we called her, was a tough lady who told my dad, "Don't call home crying if you decide that you want to get out of the military!" Despite the warning from his mother, Dad dropped out of high school and was soon on a bus to boot camp at Parris Island, South Carolina, next to a lot of "country white boys" and his cousin Sonny.

I began recognizing early in my life that my dad was a very determined person who would not let anything or anyone stand in his way, which is a trait I inherited from him. Though the plan was for them to serve together, they were separated in boot camp when Dad became ill. As a result, Sonny was deployed earlier without his younger cousin.

My father joined a division of the Navy without learning how to swim, which was ironic, because he would likely need that skill at some point. He still jumped in the water during basic training like everyone else and nearly drowned. He was allowed to continue in boot camp when a drill instructor reluctantly put the word to pass on his test. Dad was like the Parliament song as a guy who "never learned to swim!" One of Dad's favorite shows when I was growing up was *Gomer Pyle, U.S.M.C.* "Surprise, Surprise, Surprise!"

The two cousins James and Sonny would reunite after their three years of military service ended. My dad completed his GED six months after returning home; he then married my mother. The day after getting married, he took a train to Chicago with Sonny to start a new life.

My mother didn't travel with my dad because he hadn't secured a job yet, and until he secured a job, he would be staying with cousin Sonny and his sister who already lived in Chicago. Both cousins would have a variety of jobs in their early years in Chicago until, like many veterans, they secured jobs at the Post Office. Both retired from the Post Office with full benefits in their mid-50s.

The second place my parents moved into was in Englewood at 314 West Normal Parkway. This building was owned by Roscoe C. Simmons Sr., Marcella (Martha) Simmons and Bernice Kennedy Hendrix.

My father met Mrs. Hendrix at the Morrison Hotel where both were laborers. Dad worked in housekeeping and Bernice in the uniform department at the hotel. She really liked my hard-working father and would offer him food at lunchtime. She told him about an apartment building in Englewood that she and other family members had been saving to buy because their home on 35th and LaSalle was being demolished to construct the Dan Ryan Expressway.

When Bernice and her family eventually saved up enough money to purchase the apartment building, she offered my parents their pick of apartments in their building. My parents chose an apartment on the first floor of the building, which had six units. When this Black family took ownership of the building, all of the White families in the building moved out.

Roscoe C. Simmons Sr. also owned Simmons Cab Company, which was later named Sun Ray Cab Company. Before forming the cab company, Mr. Simmons and his brothers originally were operating a jitney service for people living in "The Black Belt," which is now known as Bronzeville. The cab company was formed to give the business legitimacy and expand service to other communities as Blacks were moving beyond the Black Belt in Chicago.

Another family that moved into this building was Walter and Elvira Bumpas. This young couple ended up becoming lifelong friends to my parents. My parents also became friends with Bernice's younger family members, Roscoe Simmons Jr. and his wife Mildred, who also lived in the building.

The building was located on West Normal Parkway, across from Parker High School and Wilson Junior College. That particular street was also one of the shortest streets in Chicago and ended at one of the major train lines that went into downtown Chicago.

Roscoe Jr. became a Chicago police officer, and his wife Mildred was a homemaker. Mildred also was a hairdresser for Mom for many years. The building was very family-oriented. The junior Simmons and his wife would have five children of their own. Cristal, their oldest daughter, and I are the same age and actually reconnected in college after not seeing other during our high school years.

My mother's nephew Danny Lamb lived with my parents on Normal Parkway for about two years when his mom, Stella Owens Lamb, became ill. Stella was my mom's oldest sibling. Because my sisters and I had not been born, yet many people thought Danny was my parents' first child. People would give Dad weird looks when they saw this little red-headed, fair-skinned child in the stroller, which would give my prankster dad a chuckle. My dad, like me, is pretty dark-skinned, while Danny was so fair-skinned that some neighbors (including the Black ones) thought that he was White.

I have seen many pictures of Dad with little Cousin Danny sporting bow ties and sharp outfits that my parents bought for their surrogate son. They raised him from six months old to about three years of age. Danny filled a void for my parents because they had been trying to have their own children. Like many women of childbearing age, Mom suffered multiple miscarriages in secrecy and in silence! This had to be hard for them as newlyweds. A few years later, Danny returned home to Fayetteville, Tennessee.

My parents made their first church home at a prominent church in Englewood called Antioch Baptist Church, pastored by Reverend W.N. Daniel. Reverend Daniel was a very influential Black pastor in Chicago from the 1950s to the 1970s. He invested in the Englewood community through his church and helped to build mixed and low-income housing in that neighborhood. That was an innovative thing for a church to embark on at that time.

After living for six years in Englewood, my parents moved to one of the many Chicago Housing Authority (CHA) public housing complexes in Chicago, located in Bronzeville at 2611 South Prairie Avenue, into an apartment located on the seventh floor, which was the highest floor in that building. Apartment #708 would become the gateway to our family's next step in life.

Bronzeville was named after the hue of its Black residents' skin color. Some famous residents of this community included Jesse

Owens and songstress Mahalia Jackson, who was made famous by her song "Precious Lord." Mahalia Jackson was often called by Reverend Dr. Martin Luther King Jr. to sing her marquee song on the phone to calm his nerves during the Civil Rights Movement. My mom loved that song!

The writer of the play *A Raisin in the Sun*, Lorraine Hansberry, also lived in Bronzeville. The movie version of her play starred Sidney Poitier, who reminded me of my dad when he was young. One of our family favorites growing up was watching the movie *Lilies of the Fields*, featuring Poitier as the lead character, when it came on TV at Easter. Poitier would receive an Academy Award for his role as Homer Smith. The title of this movie refers to Matthew 6:28 in the Bible: *"Consider the lilies of the field, how they grow: they labour not, neither do they spin."* The nuns in that movie reminded me of nuns I would meet later in life.

When *Good Times* premiered in 1974, it was five years after my family packed up our Ford Galaxie 500 and moved from our two-bedroom apartment out of public housing. The layout of our seventh-floor apartment was almost the same as the Evans family's fictional unit, apartment 17C at 921 N. Gilbert, in Cabrini–Green. The real Wilson apartment was home to two Tennessee transplants and their three children.

Dad's two biggest sources of pride, outside of his family, were his three years of service as a Marine and his 32 years of service as a U.S. postal worker. My mother was also proud of her many years of service as an employee of Mercy Hospital, located across the street from that project building.

Our building was one of many of the sprawling housing developments located throughout Chicago, commonly known as "the projects" or "the jets." When my parents moved into public housing, they set a goal of buying a house as soon as possible. They would achieve that goal within three years.

My parents' decision to move into public housing was to use the low rent to help them save money for a down payment and furnishings for their first home. Public housing for them was a gateway to the future, much like the Arch in St. Louis was the gateway to the West.

From the front porch of our home, we could see Mercy Hospital across the street, where my mom worked. We could also see McCormick Place, the world's largest convention center, to the east and the skyscrapers of the South Loop to the north.

South Commons condominiums were under construction one block to the west of our building. Mercy Hospital, the oldest hospital in Chicago, was the Catholic hospital where my sister Ramona Yvette was born on May 1st, 1966, in the original building, which was replaced by its current structure while we lived on Prairie. My other sister Vanessa Lynn was born earlier at Provident Hospital in April of 1965, when we lived on Normal Parkway.

In the opening credits of *Good Times*, the Els (elevated trains) running on the tracks past the Merchandise Mart over the Chicago River brought back memories. If you are from Chicago, you know the familiar roar of those trains and the squeal the wheels make while making sharp turns on the track. I literally could hear those squeals in my mind.

If I wanted to hear the real squeals of El trains, I could open up the back windows of our Prairie Street apartment, which faced south. We could hear the El trains of various lines heading to downtown Chicago, including the Red Line in the middle of the Dan Ryan expressway.

We could also see the fireworks at Comiskey Park on 35th Street when a White Sox player hit a home run. They are the true baseball team of Chicago... South Side!

That baseball park was located in the Bridgeport community just across from the Dan Ryan Expressway, an unofficial border for Black residents at that time. Black residents weren't allowed to live west of the Dan Ryan at 35th Street. Going west of 35th Street past Comiskey as a Black person on foot was very problematic.

On TV, as the names of the various actors who star in *Good Times* are revealed in the show's opening credits, the iconic Marina City with

28

its twin towers comes into view. These famous honeycomb-inspired twin towers were designed by a Jewish architect named Bertrand Goldberg. These buildings are located on some of the most expensive real estate in Chicago on the banks of the Chicago River.

Not far from where we lived, on Cermak Road, was a parcel of land on the edge of Chinatown called the Hilliard Homes, which was a public housing project also designed by Bertrand Goldberg, with a honeycomb design that mimics Marina City. They were opened two years before Marina City with a design that was supposed to take poor residents' minds off of the abject poverty that they lived in. That never quite happened!

The El, which is part of the Chicago Transit Authority (CTA), crosses over the Chicago River in the opening credits for *Good Times*. This river is one of the two water lifelines for the City of Chicago. The other is Lake Michigan, which Chicago borders on. Lake Michigan is one of the largest bodies of freshwater in the world and provides all of the drinking water for Chicago and many surrounding suburbs. The design of the City of Chicago is a rectangular grid parallel to Lake Michigan. The El is a lifeline for many of the poor in Chicago who don't have vehicles, while being shared by the rich as well.

On the banks of that same Chicago River was the site of the original settlement where a Black Haitian named Jean Baptiste Pointe du Sable would become the first non-native resident of the City of Chicago in 1781. This Black man would become known as the founder of this great city. That same El train connects to the ghettos and the most prosperous parts of Chicago. Water and railways would be historically important to the future of Chicago and its residents. At one time, Chicago was the hub for all railroads in America.

Those kids running up the block between the high rises and row houses in those opening views of Cabrini–Green in *Good Times* were literally steps from my father's part-time job at the headquarters of Montgomery Ward. This location was not far from his first postal job as a mail sorter at the Main Post Office of Chicago.

My dad had co-workers who lived in those very row houses of Cabrini–Green that we would visit from time to time. Those television images would make me crave a sandwich from Mr. Beef, a sandwich shop on Orleans Street near where those kids are playing in the opening credits of the show. My dad would bring those beef sandwiches home when he worked overtime at his job at Montgomery Ward. Chicago is famous for its roast beef sandwiches.

My family and I would watch the show over the years, and it would be hard to ignore the similarities between the stories on the show and the story of my family. The three Evans children matched the number of me and my sisters. The head of the family was named James, just like our dad. And with a name like Florida, the family matron had an unusual first name, like our mom named Alease.

In the show, the beautiful Thelma would eventually marry a person named Keith. Thelma's husband Keith would be one of the most popular characters on the show, which seems fitting, as a Keith should rule the world! Keith was a player for the Chicago Bears who injured his knee on the day of his wedding to Thelma in an accident involving J.J. The addition of his character became the basis of new storylines on the show.

I have seen the last episode of *Good Times* countless times now in reruns, and I always get a kick out of the perfect ending the writers created for the iconic show. As much as I loved the show, the ending was always a little unrealistic to me. It had the perfect ending with J.J. finally getting his big break. Keith and Thelma were having a baby, with Florida moving in to help them. That knee injury which kept Keith from playing with the Bears was miraculously cured.

During that last show, Michael was planning to move into the dorms on his college campus in his pursuit to become a lawyer. I hated how he pronounced "dormitory" in that episode because it sounded like "DomeATORY." I imagined that he probably went to Chicago State or the University of Illinois at Chicago (UIC) on a scholarship.

According to that final episode, the hugging friends Florida and Willona would again end up living in the same building when Willona and her adopted daughter, Penny, coincidently ended up moving into the same building as Thelma and Keith. That seemed like a lot of perfection after all of those years of ups and downs, and was that real life?

It is very difficult to close out any show and give viewers a sense of closure, and this show was no different. Long after that very blurry final image of Willona and Florida fades and the final applause is heard, I wondered, what happened to the Evans family? Did Keith ever help the Bears win the Super Bowl? Did Bookman keep working in the projects after his closest friends all left? Did Dyno Girl become a big hit? Did Michael ever become a lawyer? Did Thelma have a writing career or become a stay-at-home mother? Whatever happened to J.J.'s many women? That T.C. was really cute. Where did she go? Did J.J.'s prom date ever get off that heroin? How about that alcoholic family friend?

After the pot of gold is found at the end of the rainbow, that is when real life begins. When you become a young adult in this country, you have to face the fact that you need to begin defining who you are and what you are going to be. By the time you find that proverbial pot of gold, you have probably been very battle tested and will likely have to fight to keep that gold once you achieve it.

My family was no different in that once they achieved the "American Dream" of home ownership, they had to work really hard to keep it. The magic of this show was that issues were usually addressed and solved within 30 minutes, or sometimes within 60 or 90 minutes for multi-part episodes.

In August of 1969, my family made our big move into our first home on the Southeast Side in the Calumet Heights Community. It was a very beautiful community with well-manicured lawns and good schools. Our new neighborhood had a multitude of businesses and very little crime. South Jeffery was a long way from the public housing on South Prairie. Though it was a very small home of about 900 square feet, it had a huge yard. I shared my tiny bedroom with a hot water heater and the family's washer and dryer, because it was actually a utility/laundry room that doubled as my bedroom. Only a twin bed and a small desk could fit in it. My sisters shared their own room. Even though my bedroom was technically the utility room, I no longer had to share a bedroom with my two sisters.

My room was an oasis until someone had to wash clothes. That little house felt like a mansion to me and my sisters. And there were *no roaches. None.* We had roaches on Prairie. Everybody had roaches! That little room was mine and that was all that mattered!

After we moved, life was very different. Most of the people who lived in the area were White. We moved from a predominantly Black environment in the projects to become only the second Black family on 90th and Jeffery. Our home was originally owned by our White neighbors to the North, Mr. and Ms. Williams, who used the home as a related living house for their son and his wife. It sat back off the street and was even with the garages on our block. Their son and his wife moved to a bigger home (their pot of gold), so their parents sold their kids' home to my parents for the ridiculously low price of $12,000. That was still a lot of money to them in 1969. The last appraisal I saw for that home a couple of years ago was for $160,000!

We thought we had moved into the perfect neighborhood until it became apparent that our White neighbors didn't feel the same way about our family. That realization hit my parents really hard when our nice neighbors, the Williamses, put their house for sale.

My parents began to wonder about that great deal they got when Mr. and Mrs. Williams sold them their related living home, when the truth was that they were leaving the block too! This was when White flight in my neighborhood began. I realized years later that it really bothered my dad that people moved because they felt that we weren't good enough to be their neighbors.

In spite of not liking the fact that White neighbors were leaving the block because "we" had moved in, Dad loved being a homeowner and was extremely proud of accomplishing the goal of moving his family into a nice community and out of the projects. He and other Black neighbors, like the Jordans who moved in two doors south, would have impeccable green yards. The men of the houses were almost competitive about their landscaping at times. The ladies of the homes tried to have the best flowers in their flower beds in their front lawns. Mom's mother, Roberta Owens, would come to town from Nashville and make magic happen with our marigolds, zinnias and petunias. Grandma Roberta kept us in the flower game!

These new Black neighbors saved their money for years to purchase their homes, so they took pride in maintaining them. The Jordans had a beautiful large Chicago-style bungalow with stained glass windows. They had well-behaved kids, a strict father and a watchful mother, like my family. Many on the block worked for the City of Chicago. One of the eldest Jordan children worked for the post office, as did Mr. Brad, another neighbor on the block. One neighbor was a Chicago policeman.

Dad had so much pride in his yard and kept his lawn green. He watered it every day like it was the turf at the Kentucky Derby. He would rake out dead spots in the lawn and would plant some Scotts grass seed as soon as he saw a bare spot. Ace Hardware on 95th just east of Jeffery supplied his Scotts Turf Builder to make sure the dandelions didn't take over.

Dad would cut his lawn weekly with his electric mower, which, along with trimming the hedges, became my job when I got older. When we first moved in, we had an old-school manual push mower, which was some work! Dad also made sure we didn't have chipping paint on our house. Our house had white wooden siding with green trim in the front and red brick in the back.

Our neighbors, the Williamses, had a Chihuahua that used to get into our yard and run through our flowers. Mrs. Williams used to have bluish gray hair in a style almost like Marge Simpson. Mr. Williams worked at the nearby Chicago Skyway on 88th Street as a toll collector. I used to think that it was such a cool job getting to touch all that money!

I can still remember seeing that look on Dad's face when the Williamses announced that they were moving just as other White neighbors started selling their homes. They were just gone one day! As nice as our neighborhood remained even after it changed, I could tell that the White flight really irked Dad.

When the White neighbors moved away, other Black neighbors replaced them. My parents befriended our new neighbors, like the Jordans. Some of the Jordans' kids were the same age as my siblings and me, while some were much older. Mrs. Jordan would sometimes watch my sisters and me if my parents needed to work overtime to make ends meet.

Another family, the Buckners, moved next door into the Williamses' house. Mrs. Buckner become another part of that village of my youth. Sometimes she would also watch me and my sisters in times of need. Mrs. Buckner was a single mother who had a daughter named Mina, who was about 10 years older than me, and a son named Michael. She also had a niece named Tracey, about the same age as my sisters, who lived with her for a while.

The Jackson family moved in next to the Bufford family one door to the north of them. Mrs. Bufford was also a single mother, with a daughter named Tessie and a son named Marvin. He was so cool. Marvin had the coolest bike with a banana seat and a long sissy bar. It was a five-speed, which made him a baller. I remember when he got a Schwinn Continental ten-speed. Marvin could fix a bike!

Mrs. Bufford worked for John Stroger, a local ward committeeman. She used to give kids money to pass out flyers around the neighborhood for Mr. Stroger when he was running for office. Eventually, I would join the same fraternity as Mr. Stroger, Alpha Phi Alpha. Mr. Stroger would become a huge player in Chicago politics and a force to be dealt with in the Black community. My wife Denise would complete her family practice medical residency at Cook County Hospital. When we were dating, Denise would talk about how influential Mr. Stroger was at that hospital while she was training there.

Mr. Stroger became the Commissioner of Cook County, and his son Todd would later succeed his father in that same job. Todd would also join Alpha Phi Alpha, just like his father. He had to be honored when they renamed Cook County Hospital to the John Stroger Hospital after his father died. Todd Stroger became an example of a Black legacy in Chicago that would impact my vision on Black life.

This reminds me of how another prominent Black man, Mr. John Johnson, left Johnson Publishing, which he founded, to his daughter Linda Johnson Rice. This was another Alphaman who left a legacy for his children. I did not know these people personally, but you can't imagine what it was like to go downtown and see a building on some of the most expensive real estate in Chicago and know that was owned by a Black man—Mr. John Johnson.

When *Jet* and *Ebony* magazines were mailed to our home with a return address from that Michigan Avenue building, that meant something to us and to other Black families. I was truly saddened at the news when the fabled Black-owned and operated publishing company fell into bankruptcy. Eventually the building was sold. Thankfully its priceless collection of photos is safely housed in the National Museum of African American History and Culture in Washington, D.C. A prominent former NBA star recently purchased the company and is giving it new life!

Mrs. Thomas, an African-American Chicago Public School (CPS) teacher who was married to a janitor, moved in next door to us to the south. She was such a proper-speaking lady with such precise diction. She was the epitome of an old-style teacher and saw every child as a student.

I really wanted to take piano lessons, but our home was too small for a piano, plus my parents also couldn't afford one. When Mrs. Thomas heard that I wanted to take lessons, she allowed me to practice on her piano after she got home from work. I wasn't her child, but back then, a neighbor's home was considered a safe zone and an important part of a true community.

Mrs. Thomas's piano was an upright Baldwin that I used to clank away on. She was forever a teacher and tried to instruct me on the notes and the various keys, but I think the smell of cigarettes and mothballs in her house was my undoing. I was a good student when it came to books, but I was terrible on the piano. She was always very nice to me even though I never became a good piano player.

I remember how she had other lady teacher friends who came by and played bridge with her regularly. I had never heard of bridge before meeting her. The only card games I knew were spades, bid whist, war and knuckles. My parents used to be big bid whist players. When it was bid whist night at our home, there would be some Al Green played on an 8-track player and much shit-talking around the kitchen table. I remember Mr. Johnnie Walker Red making an appearance at those parties too.

Mr. James Kilcrease, an African-American Chicago fireman, lived across the alley from us. He would give me a few dollars to mow his lawn each week. He had a nice collection of "ladies' magazines" that he used to keep in his garage as well as some "drinks" that he didn't want his wife to know about. His light-colored eyes reminded me of that Black firefighter in the movie *Backdraft*. There was something about his eyes! "You go! We go!"

My parents' friends the Bumpases from Englewood moved a couple of blocks away on Constance when Walter Sr. (Big Walter) took a job at Commonwealth Edison Electric Company (ComEd) on the far East Side. They lived on the next block over from my eventual high school buddies, the twin brothers Gerard and Gregory.

My parents had been friends with Big Walter and his wife since living in the Simmonses' apartment building in Englewood on Normal Parkway. His wife, Elvira, was a homemaker. Big Walter had a friend named Jerry, a Chicago police officer who moved in across the alley from us a couple of doors down to the north. His wife was a part-time model.

Across the street lived Mrs. Blackburn, a housekeeper who worked for a Jewish writer for the *Chicago Tribune* who lived on 92nd and Cregier or Bennett. He owned that home and the one on "The Hill." I used to cut the grass across the street and that of her employer who lived on "The Hill."

I saw all kinds of Black professionals and working-class Black people growing up in that community. I also have some very vivid memories of the excuses that White neighbors made when they moved as more Blacks began moving into the area. Many White people have no clue how that makes Black people feel. You are moving to Oak Lawn because...?

Pill Hill was an affluent community two blocks southwest of our home, named after the Jewish doctors and pharmacists who used to live there. Mrs. Blackburn's boss was one of the last Whites to move from Pill Hill. As Whites left Pill Hill, affluent Blacks moved into the nice homes with big yards. One family actually had an elevator in their home. Another home had a car wash in it. Those were some fancy homes!

Pill Hill eventually had Black doctors and lawyers. There were Black school principals and business owners there as well. Tyrone Davis, a '70s singer, lived in that community. The Leak family, very prominent Black morticians, lived in that community as well. Future actress LisaRaye McCoy also lived on Pill Hill. Many remember her as Diamond in the movie *The Players Club*.

Another Pill Hill resident was the owner of Chi-Sound Records, Carl Davis. He produced many soul groups from the 1970s including his neighbor Tyrone Davis and the Chi-Lites. A neighborhood buddy I played basketball with, who became a dentist like me, also grew up on Pill Hill. His parents were both educators, and his brother became an accountant.

Chicago Cubs baseball player Ernie Banks also lived on Pill Hill. When I was a young boy, we young fans of baseball used to go by Mr. Banks's house hoping to get him to sign our baseball cards, but he was never home as he was often traveling with his team. When we kids rang the doorbell at Mr. Banks's house, his wife used to run us off. She was probably annoyed with all of the kids always ringing her doorbell.

In Chicago, we have two baseball teams, the Cubs and the White Sox. It is customary to be a fan of just one of them. It's not that Cub fans hated Sox fans or the other way around, but Chicagoans are very tribal. Who is a true South Sider? No ketchup on a real Chicago hot dog. Catholic League vs. Public League, etc. In general, people from the South Side tended to be Sox fans, while Northsiders were usually Cub fans.

Growing up, I was a fan of both teams, but I leaned toward the Cubs until I was six or seven years old. I loved Jack Brickhouse, who was a Cubs announcer on Channel 9. I used to really like José Cardenal, a Cuban player for the Cubs who had a big Afro. But at that age, I was a little conflicted and had baseball cards from both teams. I had a Minnie Miñoso card and a Billy Williams card.

I loved so many things about our new home and our neighborhood. I was so excited that Cubs star Ernie Banks lived about four blocks from our new house. Also, folks on Pill Hill gave out good candy at Halloween. Those things were important to a Black kid at that time.

As I began to study my teams more closely, I changed baseball affiliations in the fourth grade. The first reason was Mrs. Banks was a little grouchy towards us kids. Reason number two was that my new Catholic school had the tradition of giving students with good grades or perfect attendance free tickets to Sox games. Between those free tickets and the grouchy Mrs. Banks, the choice became obvious! Go Sox!

The impact of living in that community was undeniable in my life. While attending the University of Illinois at Chicago (UIC), I would later make friends with Carla, Cheryl and Charles (Chuck Jr.) and find out that they grew up a few blocks from me in one of those beautiful homes on "The Hill." Growing up in that neighborhood made me want to go to college. One reason that I became a dentist was because my new college friends' father was my first Black dentist when we first moved to the community. He was one of the first Black dentists on the South Side, and I was inspired as a kid when I saw him in his dental office.

His daughter Cheryl would become a dentist and take over her father's practice on nearby Stony Island after she graduated from dental school. Another Black legacy! She also became President of the

Chicago Dental Society, which is the largest component branch of the American Dental Association.

Future City of Chicago Treasurer Stephanie Neely also lived on Pill Hill. Her family owned a number of Shell Gas stations on the South Side, including one on 87th and Stony Island that my Dad frequented regularly because it was Black owned. I remember hearing when I was growing up that Stephanie owned a horse. A Black person in Chicago who owned a horse was an exciting idea to me at the time.

Micah Materre, a news reporter for Channel 9 (WGN-TV), is another person who lived on Pill Hill. My sisters attended Elizabeth Seton Catholic High School a few years behind her. Her younger sister Gloria would become an attorney. Their father was an insurance broker in the community with an office on Stony Island.

There were just so many examples of successful people from the community that I roamed as a youth. Thankfully, I had so many role models, which made me realize that I had a lot of career options.

Another neighborhood buddy, Nate, and his sister Angie lived in that community. Their parents were an accountant and a teacher. Both of my friends became very successful in their chosen fields. My twin high school buddies lived across the street from them with their two sisters, and their parents were an educator and a butcher. I became good friends with their sister Cathy while attending Saints Peter and Paul Grammar School. She is currently an obstetrician/gynecologist.

That neighborhood, with its multitude of educated and working-class people, was very influential in how the youth in the community viewed education and Black success. I always knew that Blacks could be successful because I saw it firsthand. In many ways, Pill Hill was like a Black Beverly Hills. I could see my future self when I looked at the successful Blacks with beautiful homes, cars and families in my community. One neighbor owned a DeLorean while another owned an Excalibur.

Whether they were mail carriers, teachers, plumbers, business people or a variety of other professions, I was a witness to the true potential of Black people. I also noticed that most of the families that I got to know during that period of my life had two parents who worked as a team, like my parents. That experience made marriage another future goal.

Change was coming when the community became virtually all Black by the end of the 1970s. Most troubling was how neighborhood businesses began to close towards the end of that decade as more Blacks moved into the community. Services weren't kept at the same level as when Whites were in the majority. Some of the neighborhood grocery stores seemed not to be as clean, and things like fruits, vegetables and meats seemed to have a poorer quality.

Pill Hill was literally located on an actual hill and became the high-end community for Blacks who lived on the South Side. Chatham, a similar neighborhood, was located just to the West. The singer Mahalia Jackson was one of the first Blacks to integrate that community. The owners of Johnson Products also lived in Chatham, as did my friend Janice Boutte and her family. Her father, Alvin Boutte Sr., was a pharmacist and co-founder of Independence Bank, which was once the largest Black-owned bank in the U.S.

Though it was located a couple of blocks from our home, people made it clear that our home on 90th and Jeffery Boulevard was not a part of Pill Hill. There was a bit of classism and colorism at play in the community at times, and Chatham and Pill Hill had an unfortunate history of both.

The Eastern border of the rectangular Pill Hill community extended to Euclid Street, which ran north to south. The western border was East End, which also ran north to south. These two streets are parallel to one another. Jeffery Boulevard is the adjacent parallel street immediately east of Euclid. Stony Island was parallel to East End and one block West. Jeffery Boulevard and Stony Island, with their busy streets, served as walls for the quiet residential streets located within Pill Hill. Both of those streets are busy arteries on the South Side with a lot of traffic and CTA bus routes.

Jeffery Boulevard actually begins where Lake Shore Drive ends on the South Side. I ended up living just off Lake Shore Drive like the Evans family when they moved from the projects. The northern border of Pill Hill is roughly 90th or 91st Street, running east to west, and the southern border is the northern side of 93rd Street running East to West. 93rd Street is a busy bus route that insulates the southern border of Pill Hill. Homes located on the South side of 93rd are not a part of Pill Hill, according to the way it was explained to me as a young person.

By the Bicentennial year of 1976, Pill Hill was virtually all Black. Other nearby communities of Jeffery Manor, Chatham, Avalon Park, South Shore and South Chicago were also going through this transformation. Our home was located in the Calumet Heights community, and Pill Hill was a carve-out of that community. Jeffery Manor was the community south and east of the 95th Street viaduct on Jeffery. These areas all became predominately Black by the end of the 1970s.

The adjacent community to the east of Calumet Heights is South Chicago. This community was the location of my future grammar school, Saints Peter and Paul, on East 91st at Exchange Street. That community became mixed with Mexican-Americans and Blacks during the '70s. The far Southeast Side community of Hegewisch just to the east of South Chicago was mainly White and was off limits to Blacks at that time.

The Jewish center on 91st and Jeffery became the Benjamin O. Davis Center around 1972, named after a famous Black Air Force officer. Its swimming pool seemed to have more Blacks in the water over time. Markon's, a fine restaurant owned by Mel Markon, was next to the center, and it mysteriously burned down in the early 1970s. The owner, a famous Chicago restaurateur, then relocated the business to the North Side of the city.

Bethany Lutheran Church, located on the east side of Jeffery at 91st Street, was the first church my family joined when we moved into our new home. Its White membership began to decline throughout the '70s. I would later notice that Catholic church is very similar to Lutheran church. My first neighborhood grammar school, Joseph

Warren Public School, was located across the street from Bethany on 92nd Street and would have a very different student body by 1976 as well.

Robert A. Black Grammar School was a public school located on 91st and Euclid. It was a selective enrollment school (also known as a magnet school) and a feeder school to Whitney Young High School, one of the first magnet high schools in Chicago. My parents tried to get me into Robert A. Black with no luck, even though I had the grades and the school was on the next block from our home.

On the east wall of that school, adjacent to its parking lot, used to be a spray-painted rectangular box with an "X" in it mimicking a strike-out zone. Local batters would receive pitches and do their best Reggie Jackson swing to jack a baseball out of there. In front of this strike-out box, many a lead ball has made its way across Jeffery during games of strike-out from that location.

Another popular game, played at garage-mounted basketball hoops, was Varsity, aka 21. Players were challenged to be the first to score 21 points during a half-court game by single points. The game utilized imaginary and arbitrary goal and free throw lines and had very liberal rules on personal fouls. Punk fouls were not to be called.

Because of Chicago politics, many Black teachers in CPS were carving out seats in selective enrollment schools for their kids at schools like Robert A. Black and Walt Disney on the North Side of Chicago. Education is never equal, even in a changing Black neighborhood.

Another very important place in my youth was Stony Island Park, located two blocks North on Jeffery across the street from Chicago Vocational High School (CVS). We young people used to go to that park to play Piggy. This was the name of a popular hood version of softball where players would call numbers like "piggy one," which indicated your desire to be the pitcher. Piggy was a game where players wanted to get a bat and pop that softball as far as they could. In that park we also played basketball and tennis, and we would run around that rectangular park for exercise. The park was later renamed to Jesse Owens Park. Mr. Owens was a famous member of Alpha Phi Alpha and a track star who defied Adolf Hitler by winning four gold medals in the 1936 Olympic Games. 1936 was the same year my mother and father were born.

A big blow to the neighborhood came in 1982 when Fun Town, a popular amusement park on 95th and Stony Island Avenue, closed down. "Hey Momma, hey Daddy, let's go to Fun Town! Fun Town, Fun Town, Fun Town for the kids and you… 95th and Stony Island Avenue… Fun Town!" I loved that commercial when it played on WVON and WJPC. That jingle was written by Mr. Richard Pegue, a DJ at WVON at the time. Fun Town was literally the last amusement park located in the city limits of Chicago. Its closing was the end of an era, which coincided with the rise of Great America in suburban Gurnee, Illinois.

WJPC was an AM radio station owned by John Johnson, founder of Johnson Publishing Company. Mr. Johnson, a member of Alpha Phi Alpha Fraternity, published the magazines Ebony, *Jet* and *Ebony Jr.* Tom Joyner, also known as the "Fly Jock," began his radio career at WJPC.

WVON or the Voice of the Negro was the most popular Black radio station in Chicago, owned by the founders of Chess Records, Leonard and Phil Chess. It had a cast of DJs known as the "Good Guys." Herb Kent was a legendary DJ at WVON, as was Yvonne Daniels, one of the first Black female DJs in the nation. Herb Kent is in the Guinness Book of World Records for the longest career in radio.

WLS-AM was the most powerful AM radio station in Chicago, with one of the strongest signals in the nation. It had a Top 40 format similar to Dick Clark's American Bandstand, which aired on their television counterpart: WLS TV Channel 7, the ABC affiliate in Chicago.

WLS had a popular DJ on the radio station named Larry Lujack. He used to have a segment called "Animal Stories" that featured wild stories about animals. This show likely inspired me and my family to have a variety of pets in our little house. The Wilson family housed turtles, hamsters, birds, fish, cats and even a rabbit. Keep in mind that we lived in the city. This is probably why my sister Vanessa wanted to be a veterinarian when she was younger. The most unusual pets in the Wilson home were our pet ducks.

In the 1970s, there was a children's television show called *Ray Rayner and His Friends* that used to come on WGN channel 9 in the mornings before *Romper Room*, another children's show. We kids would watch these shows before venturing out to school each morning. *Ray Rayner* was also the show where school closings were announced during bad weather, so we kids would eagerly listen to see if our school's name was called.

The show featured a jumpsuit-clad Ray Rayner with crazy hats and a bunch of post-it looking notes pinned to his jacket. The show had comedy segments and showed Bugs Bunny cartoons. His co-star was a four-foot dog puppet named Cuddly Dudley and a live duck named Chelveston. That show made mornings before school great.

My sisters and I really wanted a duck like Chelveston. Goldblatt's, a famous retailer at the time, used to sell live ducks and rabbits at Easter. One year, my sisters and I convinced our parents to get two baby ducks from the Goldblatt's department store on 91st and Commercial across the street from Saints Peter and Paul School. We then brought our new pets home with a little plastic swimming pool like the one Chelveston the Duck had on the show. We fed our feathery friends lettuce and let them run around our big yard. Those little cute yellow guys became big as hell by the end of the summer.

Because we bought them in the early spring at Easter, it was warm enough to keep them outside in a shed in our yard. But when Fall arrived, we had to bring them into the warmer house. Ducks are loud and kind of stink, so as a result, Dad wasn't feeling the little pets when we moved them into the house. Once they were in the house, I kept them in the wash basin next to the washing machine in my bedroom.

By Thanksgiving, Dad was really tired of the noise and smell of those ducks and happened to mention this problem to his friend "Big Walter." Big Walter said his mother, Lavelle, could help with the little darlings, who were really pretty big by then. Big Walter said that his mom would keep the ducks at her place in Englewood, so the problem was solved.

My father seemed so overjoyed, and we kids were happy, believing that we could visit our little feathery pals on the weekends. A couple of days later, my sisters and I asked to see our ducks, but were stunned when Dad told us that our ducks had been served as dinner! We cried!

We had great memories in that "Little House on The Prairie." The nickname for our house was a play on the fact that we moved from Prairie Avenue and the house was so far off the street from the other homes on the block that it was almost in the wilderness. *Little House on the Prairie and The Waltons* were two of my favorite television shows growing up.

"KEEPING YOUR HEAD ABOVE WATER, MAKING A WAVE WHEN YOU CAN!"

Our 1st house on South Jeffery in the
Calumet Heights Community of Chicago, 60617

CHAPTER 4
"Florida's Favorite Passenger"

Originally aired May 23, 1979

In the years since my family left public housing, I have learned that many people have a lot of misconceptions about people who live or have lived in the projects. One truism is that ALL parents love their kids regardless of where they live. Parents in the projects are no different.

Most people living in the projects while we were residents were very hard workers. It also was the case that most residents in public housing had low paying or unskilled labor jobs.

When we lived in public housing, people often worked in retail at stores like Montgomery Ward and Sears. Lake Meadows Shopping Center on 35th and Martin Luther King Drive was a center for local jobs in Bronzeville, with stores like Goldblatt's and Walgreens.

Drexel Bank, which was our family bank, was also located in Lake Meadows. Mercy Hospital was one of the biggest employers for Bronzeville and Bridgeport residents. The first Mayor Daley and his family used Mercy as their family hospital as they were devout Roman Catholics.

During this time, my mom's friend Elvira worked at another Chicago-based retailer called Spiegel, a national catalogue store located in the nearby Bridgeport community on 35th Street. This store was a short distance from Comiskey Park, the home of the Chicago White

Sox. Spiegel had some of the best Christmas catalogues, though the ones from Sears and Montgomery Ward were my personal favorites.

The mayor of Chicago, Richard J. Daley, and his family, including his son Richard M. Daley, lived in Bridgeport. Richard M. Daley would also eventually become the mayor of Chicago. He would become the longest-serving mayor of the City of Chicago with 22 years in office, which was a year longer than his father.

As recently as the 1990s, Bridgeport was a community where Blacks were not allowed to be west of 35th past Comiskey Park after dark. Blacks were frequently harassed on 35th Street right near Mayor Daley's house.

In the 1970s, Chicago's numerous public housing projects essentially became places where the residents were mainly poor and Black. For those who lived in public housing, White working-class communities like Canaryville, Little Italy, the Gold Coast and Back of the Yards seemed like another world.

It was often the case that Black residents in public housing did all the right things in life, like their working-class White counterparts, but just didn't get the same opportunities. The difference in the outcomes was often solely race-based.

Chicago is truly a city where systemic racism has been alive and well for generations. The same police force protecting the street corners around Comisky Park who are ultra- protective of White community members leaving the ballpark have a different attitude when they see Black fans.

Black residents from the projects often dreamed of leaving the concrete confines of those high-rise mouse traps (pun intended). People of all races on the outside often looked down at people in the "jets" and passed judgment about why they lived there and how they ended up there.

Outsiders were usually WRONG about the people who lived in the projects. Folks who did not live in the projects often believed that the people living in them were just lazy or just wanted to live off of public assistance. Nothing could be further from the truth!

All communities have similarities that bind them. Residents of the impoverished Cabrini–Green projects could just look out of their window into the Gold Coast of Chicago where many of the wealthiest people in the city lived. That had to be tough!

Chicago was literally a "Tale of Two Cities" within two blocks of one another. It was the best of times for residents in the Gold Coast or Lincoln Park but the worst of times in South Side communities like Englewood and the West Side of Chicago.

The first female mayor of Chicago, Jane Byrne, decided that for a short time that she would move from the Gold Coast into Cabrini–Green in a publicity stunt to help her reelection bid. Most people saw that maneuver for what it was, which was a feeble attempt to pander for the Black vote while seeming to be a compassionate person for White voters.

A White stay-at-home mother from the fancy North Shore Chicago suburb of Northbrook has the same problems with her children as a working-class Black single mom from the impoverished Roseland community on the South Side of Chicago.

Mothers and fathers in the projects didn't always have grassy lawns for their kids to play on. Sometimes there were bad apple neighbors. There were occasional burning smells from down the hall that were not always garbage in the incinerator. If you have ever lived in the projects, you know that distinctive burning garbage smell when compared to the smell of marijuana.

Most of our neighbors in CHA (Chicago Housing Authority) at 26th and Prairie were really nice people. Kids rode bikes, and there were often barbecues in the playground during the summer. Transistor radios could be heard blasting the latest Earth, Wind & Fire song on WVON radio AM 1450, the Voice of the Negro featuring Herb Kent. The Good Humor ice cream truck with its familiar melody would roll into the parking lot and the kids would gather to purchase their treats.

Girls jumped double dutch on the sidewalk. Men could also be seen working on their cars in the parking lot. If you looked up from the playground, you could see mothers sitting in chairs on the various floors reading magazines or playing cards while looking down and watching the children.

Over the years, public housing began to change. As the '70s progressed into the early '80s, there was an increase in divorced mothers and single mothers with children moving into public housing. Many of these ladies were on public assistance or welfare, and the new mothers often needed federal programs such as WIC. Most people in the jets became very familiar with powdered milk and the staple "government cheese."

Between the 1970s and 1980s, there was a decrease in people getting married in society in general. Black single mothers led homes that tended to struggle more than their White counterparts because White single mothers tend to have more access to resources.

The system was set up so women on public assistance would also be penalized if an unmarried man lived with them. If a visiting social worker should find evidence of illegal co-habitation, a resident could be evicted. If your spouse was convicted of a crime, they were not allowed to live in your unit.

Good Times had an episode with a White social worker who checked on Willona while she was trying to adopt a young lady named Penny. The challenges of Black adoption are highlighted in the episode. Social workers played an important role in helping these new nontraditional families navigate the challenges of their personal situations.

It was not uncommon for overworked social workers to routinely do spot checks through housing projects in an attempt to uncover women who were harboring boyfriends or criminal male relatives in their apartments, which could result in evictions.

The popular blaxploitation movie *Claudine*, featuring Diahann Carroll and James Earl Jones, illustrated the problematic issues and restrictive rules faced by poor families living on welfare. The rules of public housing created a paradox that systematically made it impossible for many unmarried men to be responsible for their children, because they could not legally live in the same apartment as their children with women they often were not married to.

Sometimes neighbors would act as spies and report infractions to get an enemy down the hall kicked out of an apartment. How many times on *Good Times* did Bookman hold over the Evanses' heads the threat of eviction for some petty infraction? Regressive rules and regulations created an element of constant fear in Black families in those subsidized apartments.

The cousin from down South looking for a job or that son recently released from prison would not legally be able to reside with his relatives in public housing. Black families tried to stick together in a system that was designed to separate and destroy them. Often this system broke Black families!

The world of 1974, when *Good Times* premiered, was so different from the world of 2021. Even in public housing, Black people had a tendency to be more village oriented. It was about the collective. It was about community. It was also about everyone "Movin' on up." As time moved forward, the village's hands would be tied by even more rules and regulations, which would lead to devastating and continual problems in the Black community.

My parents also understood the importance of community and creating partnerships with neighbors. There were countless times when my parents left me and my sisters in the care of our neighbor Mrs. Milton down the hall so they could go to work. Mrs. Milton provided daycare virtually for free so that my parents could work. How many single mothers struggle with childcare today?

Head Start was a federally funded program created to help disadvantaged youth get an educational jumpstart before kindergarten, and it also helped many people with children in public housing. In a twist of fate, I would eventually end up being kicked out of Head Start because they claimed my parents made too much money for me to stay in the program. My parents, between all of their jobs, probably made around $18,000 to $20,000 in total. Too much indeed! What a joke! As a result, I attended kindergarten at nearby St. James Catholic School. That change was actually a blessing in disguise!

When my family moved into our new home on Jeffery Street, I would often remember what living in the projects was like. I especially remembered how important the elevator was: since we lived on the seventh floor, we used the elevators every day. When the elevator didn't work, this would mean walking up and down seven flights of stairs! The expression "Waiting on Otis" had a double meaning in our high-rise project building. It could mean simply waiting for the elevator, or it could also mean waiting on the Otis elevator repairman.

Riding project elevators required a special set of skills at times. You had to learn at a young age how to pry the doors open if the elevator stopped. Also, you couldn't be scared to climb out of the elevator if it got stuck between floors, because if you didn't master climbing out of a stuck elevator, you would have to wait a long time to be rescued.

Improper execution of a stuck elevator escape could result in you falling to your death down the elevator shaft. One of the weird things I remember is the giant spring that you could see at the bottom when you looked down the shaft. You also needed to have the ability to hold your breath during most elevator rides if there was the customary urine puddle on the floor.

For whatever reason, very vivid memories of the elevator in our old apartment building come to mind when watching one particular episode of *Good Times* titled "Florida's Favorite Passenger." In this two-part episode, Florida works as a bus driver and becomes very close to Larry Baker, one of the riders on her bus route. Florida brings Larry home to wait for his mother because his mother did not pick him up after school. While waiting for Larry's mother, Florida determines that the very bright Larry has an undiagnosed hearing problem.

When Ms. Baker shows up to pick up Larry from the Evanses' apartment, Florida casually mentions her observation about Larry's hearing. Initially, the overwhelmed single mom with two jobs is offended and angered by what she perceives as Florida's interfering in her son's health.

After the negative encounter between the two mothers in the apartment, Ms. Baker rushes out of the apartment angry. She then asks Larry to push the elevator button to summon the elevator. While Larry is waiting for his mother at the elevator, the elevator doors open up behind him with no elevator in sight.

Because of his hearing difficulties, Larry can't hear the shouts from his mother and Florida imploring him not to step back as his back is toward the open elevator shaft. Larry nearly falls down the exposed elevator shaft!

Thankfully, Larry doesn't fall into the elevator shaft. By the end of the episode, the overwhelmed Ms. Baker ends up accepting the Evans family's help with her son. Florida even volunteers to take Larry to the doctor to have his hearing checked. Ms. Baker was like many working poor parents who had two jobs but couldn't afford to take off work to take a child to the doctor and likely had no health insurance.

Having multiple low-paying jobs was not at all unusual for the working poor living in public housing. Most residents at that time had jobs, but were working poor. In 2021, many people who work for Walmart, the largest employer in America, are also working poor on some form of public assistance. There are many teachers and others with college degrees forced to supplement their income by driving for Uber or Lyft because they are paid low wages relative to the cost of living. The lack of fair living wages is how many end up in public housing or homeless.

Access to healthcare is also impacted by one's wealth or employment situation. When we were younger, my mother used to take my sisters and me to Cook County Hospital once a year to access free healthcare on go to the doctor day. Our annual routine would require Mom taking off work and getting us, sometimes by bus, to our annual checkup at "The County."

My parents technically weren't destitute, but they were the working poor in many ways. Mom might have believed that being poor was an attitude, but being short on money was a real thing! Every bit of overtime or money from a second job was needed, even while living in subsidized housing. Free and/or low-cost healthcare helped our family make ends meet.

As a current healthcare provider, I have learned firsthand about the importance of the role of mothers in ensuring families' access to healthcare on a regular basis. This is not meant to be sexist, but the reality is that often mothers are the directors of their family's healthcare. I have seen this firsthand in my role as a general dentist.

When I was growing up, Mom was old school when taking her kids to the doctor and dentist. This meant that we had to comply with anything the doctor asked us to do at an appointment. None of that "asking the child if the doctor can do XYZ" crap that some "modern" parents do. No do-overs at another appointment!

My mother was not going to take off another day from her job because one of us didn't want to get a measles vaccination or get some blood drawn. When one of those County nurses stuck that big needle in our arm, we had to suck it up! They didn't use cute little needles like they used for ear piercings at Claire's (a jewelry and accessories store) for our vaccinations.

We would go from room to room in a military exam style while getting everything looked at, tapped on or stuck with some needle. We couldn't complain or "act a fool" because something hurt. Once it was over, it was time to hit the road, Jack! What you say?

In the "Florida's Favorite Passenger" episode, Florida steps up to help a young boy who has medical needs that his family didn't know about. In the beginning, the mother rejects the notion that the village that was trying to help her and her son because of her own pride.

That episode also highlighted how people can really work hard and still not have access to all that they need. Helping a neighborhood kid is something my own mother would do for another child, but times have changed!

The village back then was extended to people in need, whether you were related to them on not. There have been many times when my parents extended their village to family members in times of need.

Over the years, my parents took in many of my cousins, aunts and uncles at different times to help them get their starts in life while living on limited resources themselves. When my parents took in my cousin Danny, his family couldn't afford to send money to help pay for his room and board, so my parents spent their own money to help out.

"Florida's Favorite Passenger" showed how neighbors or even bus drivers were part of the village. Florida suspected that Larry Baker had problems with his hearing and felt compelled to tell his mother about the problem. Who does that these days?

My sister Vanessa was like Larry in that she was born deaf in one ear, which was undiagnosed for a while. She also had very unique eyes, with one very bright blue eye and one brown one. When she was in grammar school, silly classmates made fun of her eyes. Vanessa was always a good student, but my mother picked up that she seemed to struggle with her class assignments.

Eventually, Mom had Vanessa's hearing checked, and it was discovered that she was deaf in one ear. My sister had an undiagnosed hearing problem just like Larry! During this time, my mother had a number of friends who were also parents at my sister's school who showed compassion to my sister. They wouldn't let my sister be bullied, even if she was not their child.

Mom was always inviting some of the unpopular kids, including bullies from school, to our home to hang out. She understood how children's self-esteem can be destroyed early in life by bullying and cruelty. Mom always demonstrated understanding and compassion to all of the children who came to our home, including the mean ones!

It wasn't until my sister was well into adulthood that my parents found out that she had Waardenburg Syndrome. People with this disorder can be born with unique eye colors and deafness, and also experience premature graying. My sister had been graying since high school and had the very obvious and unique eye coloring that caused her to be teased a lot in school.

Mom really didn't think much about her daughter's eyes because her family, the Owens family, had many sets of unique eye colors.

55

Her own father Collier (Carl Owens Sr.) had eyes that were known to change colors from blue to gray when he became angry. Mom's sisters, my aunts Betty Owens Jackson and Mildred Owens Thomison, had green and hazel eyes respectively.

Because of her unique eyes, my sister was featured in both the *Chicago Defender* and *Jet* magazine. Somehow my cousin Shana Ward made this photo shoot instead of me. The number one son never made it to the big time of *Jet* magazine! Making *Jet* was a big deal back in the day.

When I watched "Florida's Favorite Passenger," I remember thinking that Larry looked just like me. He had the same lopsided Afro, big eyes and slightly bucked teeth. I used to love Afro Sheen and put a lot of work into that Afro!

When Florida challenged Larry's mother to get his hearing checked out, you sensed the resentment this proud single mother had during the confrontation. She believed that Florida was looking down on her as a parent, but in reality, Florida was just trying to be a village to one of its future warriors.

It was not Florida's intent to make Ms. Baker look bad, but she wanted to make it clear she understood how tough raising a child alone could be. She wanted to make it clear that there was a village that was willing to give a helping hand. Parents in the ghetto truly tried to provide for all of their needs, but help was often needed.

It would have been easy to write Ms. Baker off as an uncaring and abusive mother, but her character was allowed to develop and show her humanity and vulnerability. She was simply a woman overwhelmed by life, trying to make it to the next day. She mistook Florida's kindness and concern for condescension and disdain. In the end, Ms. Baker realized that they were just two mother hens who cared deeply for their children, and that Florida was just offering a hand up, not a hand out.

The moral of this episode was that even in the poverty of the projects, there was a loving village willing to help out a neighbor. In the hood, there are many Larrys in need and just as many mothers like

Florida Evans. The working poor may not have money, but they do have love to share with others in need.

Coaches, priests, teachers, Cub Scout Den mothers or fathers on the block willing to pick up the kids from the circus, performed this role and still do. I will always remember how my mother was often that community mother when we were growing up.

Mom always volunteered to be one of the chaperones at school. Because of my mother, our home was the community hangout for kids on our block. Kids often came by our house and hung out in our big yard and played games for hours. At times, our home looked like the United Nations with kids of various races in our house. Even though my parents talked about racism, they wanted us to be around all types of people.

There was another episode of *Good Times* where the kids participated in a carnival. My sisters and I once had a fundraising carnival in our yard for muscular dystrophy. A popular children's television show in Chicago on Channel 32, The BJ and Dirty Dragon Show, used to encourage kids to have these yard carnivals to raise money for the condition.

Bill Jackson (BJ) was an artist who hosted the show. It was a children's show with a cast of characters including a mountain of clay mounted on a moving pedestal named "The Blob." The show had many puppets including the Dirty Dragon and the Lemon Joke Kid. I loved that show because it would have segments where BJ drew cartoons.

The BJ and Dirty Dragon Show provided party packets for the carnivals. Our carnival was a lot of fun! We had a little pool that used to be for our ducks, which we used to bob for apples. We had some other games and a piñata that I made from papier-mâché. We charged a little fee at the entrance to our yard and racked up a lot of coins! We took the money down from the carnival to the Channel 32 studio in our car. BJ was in the street collecting the money we raised, and I got to meet him. He was wearing his famous derby, but no Blob or Lemon Joke Kid was with him.

My mom wanted her kids to understand that the village is sometimes bigger than friends and immediate family, so she stressed that making a difference could include being charitable to others in need. My family often had a yard full of neighborhood or school mates from Saints Peter and Paul. Mothers during those years used to really look out for the kids in the neighborhood as every child deserved the kind of love Florida showed Larry on that show. I will never forget the love shown to me by a lifetime of mothers who kept me safe.

Mrs. Karen Fields and Mrs. Elvira Bumpas, two of Mom's closest friends, were among those mothers I would benefit from in my youth. Mrs. Fields was a White woman married to a Black man, but the color of her skin barely mattered. The relationship my mom had with her friend Karen helped to show that not all Black/White relationships were confrontational. After the racial bullying I experienced at my first grammar school., I needed to see that! Mrs. Fields was such a great wife and mother who reminded me of my own mother.

My parents still stressed the importance of getting to know people for who they are on the inside, not the color of their skin. In spite of some of the negative things I have experienced at the hands of *some* Whites, I try to be fair with everyone I encounter.

I will always remember Mrs. Fields just being one of my mother's really nice friends. She and her husband had three daughters, Danielle, Jennifer and Laura. Mrs. Fields was one of those sweet moms who came into my life and taught me a lot about how there are nice people in every race. It was so important for her to be in my life so that I could learn to appreciate the person, not the color.

I have heard stories about the hell she caught at times for being married to a Black man, but I always saw her as a loving wife and mother and a wonderful role model. She was one of those mothers who protected my sisters when my mother was not around at school. I appreciate how the Fields family and other people in the village helped to teach me that race is the least important factor in a person's humanity.

In spite of my experience with Mrs. Fields, I still needed to learn more about the complexities of my own views on race. While in high school, I got a job at the University of Chicago Hospital and made a new friend named Janice Pierson. My friend and I used to have a lot of conversations about race at lunch.

I had never met Janice's parents, so I *used* to express some very interesting opinions about race and interracial relationships to this Black co-worker. Even though I had personally observed very successful interracial relationships, I was still a little skeptical about them. My friend would teach me a big lesson!

One day, I mentioned to Jan that I made extra money cutting grass, and she said that her father was unable to cut her family's lawn and it would really help her out if I could do it. We are talking money, so I was onboard for this side job! As it turns out, she lived two blocks from my Jeffery home on neighboring Clyde Street, which really made it a good situation.

The next Saturday, I walked to her family's very nice ranch home, which was only two blocks away from my house on Jeffery. When I rang the bell, this older White guy answered the door, so I was a little thrown off. I told the man that I was looking for the Pierson residence. The old White guy said, "I'm Harold Pierson."

In my head, I was like, "Oh shit! He couldn't be!" But then I could see, just past the door that he was holding open, two Black women inside who could have been twins, sitting at the kitchen table rolling in laughter.

As it turns out, this White man named Harold Pierson was my friend's dad. Jan happens to look exactly like her Black mother, but that old White man was her dad! Over the years, I would learn what a comedian her mother was and how that situation just tickled her heart. After rubbing the foolish look off my face, I cut their grass many times. That crew became some of the best people to come into my life! We still laugh about that day.

Jan's dad passed away a few years ago, and her mom passed away in 2018 after many years in a nursing home. We would share many trials and tribulations as fellow members of the club of adults caring for elderly parents. Ann Pierson was a wonderful mother to two daughters.

Jan cared for her mother constantly when she became ill toward the end of her life. As she went through that final chapter of her mother's life, I watched in awe as she sacrificed much personally to love and care for her mother while her mother slowly lost that joyfulness as dementia took her away. Jan dealt with this heartache as a physician who could do nothing to remedy the situation in spite of being a gifted healer.

There is the doctor and there is the daughter! My wife and I went through a similar experience with my mother-in-love a few years earlier when she went on for her reward. Jan and I have come a long way from our University of Chicago Hospital days. She is a great friend to my wife and me, and certainly a part of our village.

I have tried to learn the lesson to never judge a book by its cover. There were many wonderful mothers of all races in my life as a young person who really helped me to become the person I am today.

"WATCHING THE ASPHALT GROW!"

Vanessa in Jet Magazine Circa 1966

Vanessa in the Chicago Defender Circa 1966

Just lookin' out of the window

CHAPTER 5
"Michael Gets Suspended"
Originally aired March 8, 1974

As I think about life in the projects and how our lives changed when we left, I am struck by how it was all a connected journey. My parents were always trying to make our lives better. They never wanted their children to feel limited by their circumstances, though my parents did struggle financially at times.

There was a whole world to explore, and we were a part of it. Mom made sure the whole family went to all of the Chicago museums, which were world class and often had free admission. The Museum of Science and Industry, the Field Museum, the Planetarium and the John G. Shedd Aquarium were an important part of our youth.

We also went to the Ice Capades at the Chicago Stadium and the circus at the Amphitheatre on Halsted Street by the stockyards. It smelled like crap inside and outside of the Amphitheatre because of all the slaughterhouses on the surrounding street.

We also went to Lincoln Park Zoo, one of the oldest free zoos in the United States. Dr. Lester Fisher, the director of the zoo at that time, used to have really cool animal segments on the Ray Rayner show.

Dr. Fisher trained under another famous animal person named Marlin Perkins. The Perkins name might ring a bell because he used to have a nationally syndicated show called *Mutual of Omaha's Wild Kingdom.* We watched this show on Sunday evenings right before *The Wonderful World of Disney* on Channel 7.

Once, mom took my sisters and me to see the Disney movie Fantasia. I was let down by the movie because all Mickey Mouse did was wave a little baton in the air while directing the orchestra without saying a word. What? This wasn't like the Wonderful World of Disney that used to come on TV at all! There was no Jiminy Cricket! There was no singing of "When You Wish Upon a Star." Nothing!

When I think of watching that Disney show with my family on Sundays, I remember how I used to really love when *Winnie the Pooh* was the featured show. Thinking about those days makes me think about our first family trip to Disney World with all of us packed into a tiny red Ford Pinto station wagon. It was the best time for our family!

Another family tradition in those days was going downtown. Since we had only one car, we often took the bus. The Jeffery Express was on our street and was usually our route to downtown. At some point after riding the bus, we would also ride the El. At Christmas, we went downtown in the family car to see the beautiful window displays at Marshall Field's and Carson Pirie Scott.

There were also movie theaters downtown like the State-Lake and Oriental theaters. The theaters downtown always seemed nicer than the Jeffery Theater in the neighborhood, even though they still had a rat problem like the neighborhood spots. You might have to pick your feet off those sticky floors when Ben or Willard showed up! "I used to say 'I' and 'me.'"

Though Dad never attended college, he was always a well-informed person. He read two newspapers each day: the *Chicago Sun-Times* (the newspaper Whites usually favored) and the *Chicago Defender* (the Black paper). He wanted to know what was happening on the South Side of Chicago as well as what was going on in Southeast Asia. My mother and father are two of the smartest people I know. Common sense makes them smarter than many people with PhDs!

Dad is a combination of Nipsey Russell, James Evans and Sidney Poitier. Going to the lakefront was our thing. We were five minutes away from the 39th Street beach when we lived in the projects, so we spent many days at the beach. Dad would bust out a grill, call some friends and we would be at the lake having a great time.

My father had a prank that he played on visiting relatives. We would drive to the harbor by Meigs Field next to Lake Michigan with our visiting relatives, and it would be game time once we got to the harbor. Dad would pull up to the fence outside the harbor where beautiful boats were located, pick out a random boat amongst the yachts moored there and tell the visiting family member, "There is my boat!" Then they would ask, "Which one?" Dad would point out some random boat and say, "That one." When they would ask to get on "his" yacht, the boat would become unavailable because he let the crew have the day off!

We kids would be giggling like it was an episode of *Gilligan's Island* while Dad would be cracking up and winking at us. Eventually Dad would let the person in on the gag that there was no boat, and we would have a big laugh. The idea that we lived in the projects and owned a yacht was pure comedy! My play uncle Rochester and uncle Moses were both the victims of this prank at least once.

While growing up, we had subscriptions to *Ebony* and *Jet* magazines. Dad would bring home issues of *Time* and *Newsweek* as well. Dad wanted his kids to understand that though things were so much better for us growing up at that time, racism was still alive and well. My dad was really impacted by race by growing up in the Jim Crow South, especially after joining the military, which was essentially segregated during his tour of duty.

Good Times explored the many nuances of race in their dramatic episodes. In the episode "Michael Gets Suspended," Michael challenges the accepted social world view of the history of the United States by trying to explain to his White teacher that American history is racist and often excludes positive images of Blacks.

In this episode, Michael dares to challenge his teacher by informing him that America's first president, George Washington, was a slave owner. This was a subtle challenge to the sanitized version of history the White teacher was presenting. Even now, school districts in Texas are trying to remove history books in schools that have references to slavery.

As a result of challenging authority in the episode, Michael is suspended from school. As the episode progresses, Michael educates his own parents. In the Evans family, Michael would be known as the "militant midget." This episode was one of many educational moments that the audience would experience vicariously through the antics of this precocious preteen.

In another episode, Michael is again at the center of controversy when he orders literature from communist Cuba, which results in a visit by the FBI, because writing to Cuba was forbidden communication in the 1970s. James actually loses his job when FBI agents ask questions about it to his employer. This almost seems silly in today's world, as we have been working towards normalized relations with Cuba.

The episode seems to predict the future when Michael says there would be a Black president someday. Thirty-five years after that episode first aired, another Black guy with ties to the South Side of Chicago named Barack Hussein Obama would be elected as the first Black President of the United States. That sounded so far-fetched to most people viewing that show back in 1974. The additional irony is that this future Black president with a Muslim-sounding name would be the most influential person in 50 years in normalizing Cuba-US relations.

When my sisters and I were growing up, Mom and Dad were always telling us stories about growing up in the Jim Crow South back home in Tennessee, and how bad things could be at times. They would talk openly about racism in this country. Dad would recount his time in the Marines serving to protect his nation. He would become angry recounting how he and other Black soldiers had to eat, sleep and travel in separate areas from White Marines.

My father would remark about how "White boys" would look down on Black soldiers. He remembered how the poorest of Whites would look down on their Black counterparts until something broke out. At those times, they wanted "the brothers" to help them out of those situations.

When Dad was stationed in Japan, he literally experienced one of the high points in his life when his unit marched up Mt. Fuji. But upon returning from that march, he overheard White soldiers saying ignorant things about fellow Black soldiers like Blacks having tails. This really pissed him off!

In the summer of 1969, our family marched up its own mountain when we moved into our first house at the end of that rainbow. We were the second or third Black family on the 90th block of Jeffery Boulevard when we moved in. Unfortunately, our new White neighbors also thought their new Black neighbors had tails, so they began to move out of the neighborhood.

My parents, after living the last three years in public housing to save money, were finally able to purchase their own home and leave the projects. Their dream was fulfilled when they purchased a small home in a nice community with a good school system for their kids. The schools were actually within walking distance, but that short distance seemed like miles as the children in that White neighborhood showed their true colors to me.

I was in the first grade and was initially able to walk with my mom to Joseph Warren, a public grammar school. The school was a block and a half south of my home at 92nd and Jeffery. Mom was off for a few weeks, but in the fall of 1969, about two weeks into my first grade, she needed to go back to working full time to help pay the mortgage.

It was then that I started walking alone to school. I thought that walking to my new school by myself would be so cool! But that was only until other folks in the neighborhood took note of the fat little Black kid making his way to school every day all alone, and that was when the craziness began!

My parents taught me to have a procedure for emergencies and taught me to memorize my address at 9018 S. Jeffery, Chicago, Illinois 60617. I also had to remember my phone number, which was RE1-0134 or 731-0134. You had to remember the actual numbers and the exchange. All area codes in Chicago were 312, so we didn't know the multitudes of area codes Chicago has today.

Our phone number was similar to the zip code of *ZOOM*, a popular kids' television show on our PBS station, WTTW Channel 11. "Send it to ZOOM... Boston, Mass... OH TWO ONE THREE FOUR!"

To get to my school, I would cross the street at the corner of 91st Street to the Benjamin O. Davis recreation center, make a right and walk one block south past the center's swimming pool, Markon's restaurant and Bethany Lutheran Church. I would cross 92nd Street with the help of a crossing guard, then enter the doors of Joseph A. Warren Grammar School. It was here that I learned firsthand how cruel some of my White neighbors could be.

As I passed through those doors, I remember looking at mainly White faces. Most of the people didn't seem to care about my presence, but almost immediately I noticed menacing glares from some of the boys. It was here where I would first be called a "nigger," which was a shocker! I was six years old at the time, and I thought to myself, "Don't you have to be older to be one?"

Pushes and shoves on the way to the lunch room or in between classes became a daily occurrence at Warren. One of the boys used to call me "fat blackie." Over time, the shoving escalated to gut punches in the bathroom and clothes getting ripped at recess. My lunches were always getting taken from me. I was chased home every day. It was like a bad episode of *Everybody Hates Chris*.

At first, out of embarrassment, I would deny that anything was happening at school when I returned home, but Mom noticed that I was constantly coming home with rips in my Sears Husky jeans. Ripping Sears Husky jeans took some effort because those cheap pants were tough! My mother also noticed that my clothes always seemed dirty. Both of my parents knew that I wasn't a dirty kid. At that school, I was learning firsthand about that racist stuff my parents left the South to avoid.

After a while, I decided to confide in my parents that I was getting beat up at school by the White kids. The beatdowns were usually the same scenario involving two to three White boys who were either in my grade or slightly older. I was a little bigger for my age, so I suppose they felt more threatened or were just punks, which is why it was never a one-on-one confrontation. This was humiliating for a first-grader!

My parents went to meet the White principal to discuss the problem. I was also starting to struggle academically in school, which worried my parents the most. They knew that I loved school and studying, so the bad grades were out of character. By the end of first grade, it got a little better as I was only getting beat up or chased about once a week as opposed to daily.

Even though my parents constantly met with my teachers and the principal at the school, it was to no avail. My parents had one final meeting with the principal. When my dad asked, "Is there anything that could be done to protect our son?" my parents were more or less told "NO."

The school's administrator acted as if we were the problem for deciding to move into the neighborhood. They told my parents that there was nothing that they could or would do to protect me in the school. The message was received loud and clear. It was not safe to go to that school with the racist White students who were going to continue to kick my ass!

Change is tough for some people. My parents ultimately transferred me and my sisters to Saints Peter and Paul Catholic School on 2938 East 91st Street in neighboring South Chicago. They prayed that I would not get beat up there! They also prayed that they could pay the tuition!

When my parents moved into our new neighborhood, it was because there were good public schools in walking distance. The biggest irony was that they would have to spend precious money they really didn't have just to send their kids to a "safe" school that was a half an hour from our home because of racism.

"DAMN, DAMN, DAMN!"

Just lookin' out of the window

CHAPTER 6
"The Encyclopedia Hustle"
Originally aired October 29, 1974

After a couple of years of paying for Catholic school, my parents adjusted to the idea that they were going to be permanently making this extra sacrifice to educate their children and keep them safe. My parents really liked Saints Peter and Paul School, so my mother became very involved in the school. She would often act as a "class mother" or chaperone on field trips.

Mom had been working at Mercy Catholic Hospital for a while now and really appreciated Catholic education, but it was a financial strain for my parents. Her good friend Elvira Bumpas was Catholic and probably encouraged her to stay the course with Catholic education because she had two sons attending neighboring St. Ailbe Catholic School.

Neither of my parents were Catholic, so Catholic culture was foreign to them. There were many Catholic influences on my mom's job at Mercy Hospital, where she worked in the Central Supply Department sterilizing surgical instruments, and Mom really respected the CEO of the hospital, Sister Sheila Lynne. Mom also talked about how Sister Sheila really helped out the Black employees at Mercy and how she liked my hard-working Mom.

Mercy Hospital was an important financial lifeline for my family. My sisters and I have all worked at Mercy at one time or another. After obtaining a bachelor's in psychology from UIC, I worked at Mercy on their closed Mental Unit as a Mental Health Technician,

71

as did my sister Yvette. My best friend Gerard also worked at Mercy on the Mental Health Unit after securing the same degree from UIC. Previously, we worked together at the University of Chicago Hospital in the Central Supply Department while we were in high school and early in our college years.

Working at Mercy and the University of Chicago Hospital probably played a role in our eventual career choices. Gerard would eventually get a second bachelor's degree in nursing and has had a long career at the University of Chicago Hospital. I eventually earned a doctorate in dental science from UIC and became a dentist.

A psychology degree seems so academic when you read about things like Electroconvulsive Shock Therapy (ECT) being used to treat severe depression. When I took psychology classes in college, the descriptions of using electric shock on people sounded barbaric! But on the unit, I actually witnessed ECT in person and saw patients emerge immediately from a depressed stupor to a fairly lucid state. Real-life experiences help you realize that real life is complicated and is not always so black and white.

There was a period in college when my siblings and I all attended Saint Xavier College in Oak Lawn together. I originally matriculated into UIC when I graduated from high school but struggled a bit in the large public university setting, so I transferred to this small Catholic college for a while. Classes were much smaller than at UIC, and its Catholic setting just felt familiar. The years of Catholic education with its smaller, nurturing environment had slightly spoiled and underprepared me for the large public college setting where teachers could care less if you were in class.

While at Saint Xavier, I realized that I also wasn't that interested in the electrical engineering career I had been pursuing at UIC and decided that a career in healthcare was my true calling, so I started taking pre-med classes. Sister Frances Crean taught chemistry at Saint Xavier and helped rekindle my interest in pursuing a career in healthcare. I mentioned in passing to her that I really thought that I wanted to be a doctor and she responded, "Why not?" She was the second nun in my life to tell me that I was talented at something, the first being Sister Marilyn in grammar school.

While I was at Saint Xavier, I would end up in that same chemistry class with my old friend and neighbor Jan Pierson, who was also pre-med. She was taking a summer chemistry class at Saint Xavier while attending the University of Chicago full time. My sister Vanessa, who was studying to be a veterinarian at that time, also ended up in that same class. Saint Xavier was managed by the Sisters of Mercy, which also managed both Mercy Hospital and neighboring Mother McAuley High School.

I also had other possible healthcare career interests including pharmacy, dentistry and optometry. As a youth I had very uncoordinated eyes, so my parents used to take me to the Illinois College of Optometry, about 10 minutes away from our old apartment at 26th and Prairie. Working with the nice people there made a career as an eye doctor seem plausible. Dentistry was already entered into my wheelhouse of interests after meeting my neighbor Cheryl and her family at UIC, before transferring to Saint Xavier.

Medicine had a big influence on my life because of my mother. My mother was so popular at Mercy that she would often be invited to the homes of different doctors at the hospital. I enjoyed meeting the doctors and played with their children often. Conversations related to healthcare were always being discussed in our home because my mother loved Mercy Hospital. Soul singer Deniece Williams worked at Mercy before her singing career took off, and my mother would tell stories about how Ms. Williams would sing in the hallways of the hospital while working.

Mercy Hospital was really important to our family because it provided jobs, financial security and insight into the healthcare profession. My sister Vanessa is currently an occupational therapist, and she worked as a phlebotomist at Mercy while pursuing her associate's degree in occupational therapy. Though my sister Ramona is not in healthcare, her experience working on the mental health unit at Mercy and her college studies in psychology certainly help her do a better job in her current position as a Chicago police officer. Many of the calls that she deals with are people experiencing a mental health crisis.

Provident Hospital, where I was born, is a famous historically Black hospital and the site where Dr. Daniel Hale Williams performed the very first successful open-heart surgery. Dr. Williams, a Black man, was the Chief of Staff at Provident for many years. After I graduated from college, I would become a member of the Alpha Phi Alpha Fraternity in 1987 via the Iota Delta Lambda Chapter of Chicago, and Provident was the location of our monthly chapter meetings.

I would have a lot of connections to this hospital which held an important place in Black history. My good friend Cathy, who is now an obstetrician, worked at Provident, and my fraternity and chapter brother Dr. Connie Swiner, an anesthesiologist, also worked at Provident. Dr. Swiner was one of the first members to welcome me into Alpha Phi Alpha on the morning of August 30th, 1987, at 1:34 AM.

I have much to be appreciative about as a result of joining that prestigious organization. I have given much to that organization, but received much in return. Upon completion of my dental education, I enrolled in a general practice residency for one year at Michael Reese Hospital in Bronzeville. During my residency, I had a number of rotations into the various departments. When it was time to do my anesthesia rotation, who shows up but my good fraternity brother and friend Dr. Connie Swiner. He became one of my attending surgeons and trained me while not even hazing me! Very cool!

I appreciate the guidance and support that this man gave me during that trying time. Dr. Swiner allowed me as a training dentist to do some interesting things in the operating room because of our fraternal relationship. Brotherhood matters a lot to me, though I have no biological brothers. Alpha Phi Alpha has opened many doors for me in my lifetime.

Dr. Swiner is a proud graduate of Howard University's School of Medicine and hails from the "Chocolate City" also known as Washington, D.C. He was the first Black person I ever met who was a graduate of the College of William and Mary. He recently celebrated his 40th year as a member of Alpha Phi Alpha Fraternity.

Because of my membership in Alpha Phi Alpha, I would be affiliated with many impressive fraternity members in my chapter. These men would motivate me to seek personal and professional excellence. One such member was Eddie L. Jones II, who was an executive at IBM. Eddie was a graduate of Wendell Phillips in Bronzeville, the same school that Marla Gibbs and Sam Cooke attended. He grew up in Bronzeville and also attended the University of Illinois at Chicago.

Eddie carried the U.S. Olympic torch and worked on the advance security team for former U.S. President William Jefferson Clinton. Because of Eddie, I would meet Vice President Al Gore. This meeting occurred because Eddie had solicited me to be a part of the volunteer transportation crew for one of Al Gore's vice-presidential visits to Chicago. I have an official White House picture of me and VP Gore on the tarmac outside of Air Force Two at O'Hare Airport.

I knew Gore was from Tennessee, so I let him know that my parents were from Tennessee as well. During that visit I also chauffeured Donna Brazile, who would become a key political strategist in the Democratic Party. While driving her around that day, I heard some great political intrigue.

Another fellow chapter member, Dr. Waldo E. Johnson Jr., became a professor at the University of Chicago after completing his PhD at the University of Michigan. He would serve in an advisory role to his friend Barack H. Obama, our nation's first Black president. He is also a published writer. My wife and I were honored to be invited to a book signing that he held at the home of his friend Mama Kaye Wilson, who was one of the Obama children's godparents.

I still would love to meet Mr. Obama and his lovely wife, Michelle. But I still have met some great people as a result of Alpha Phi Alpha Fraternity. Mrs. Obama is a "South Side Girl" who went to Whitney Young High School. Whitney Young is a Chicago Public School, and I certainly feel I could have done well if I was a student there. Recently the gymnasium was renamed after Mrs. Obama, and she also wrote her best-selling memoir titled *Becoming*.

Every year, my Alpha chapter, Iota Delta Lambda, better known as IDL, participates in a Men's Health Fair at Provident Hospital. Provident holds a special place for me as I was born there. Dad would always talk about how radio DJ Herb Kent's then wife delivered their daughter Robbin on the same Provident ward while my mother was delivering me.

Herb Kent of WVON radio was one of my favorite DJs growing up. He was famous throughout the Chicagoland area, and I spent many years trying to meet him. Before he died, he would become the longest-running broadcaster in radio history according to the Guinness Book of World Records. He was also inducted into the Radio Hall of Fame. He set the standard for radio DJs before computers performed radio programming. Mr. Kent was a Chicago icon and was nicknamed "The Mayor of Bronzeville," where he lived as a youth. Just before he died, I discovered that Mr. Kent actually worked out at Body by Ivory, which was the same South Suburban health club where I worked out at for years. Though it was a small club, I was never there at the same time as Mr. Kent.

I spent half of my adult life trying to meet my first real radio DJ and would always miss him at his various appearances. I finally got a chance to meet him at a South Suburban Jack and Jill Chapter event where the members were having a fundraiser. On that day, Mr. Kent had a bad cold, but I still asked him to sign a copy of his autobiography that I happened to have with me. I was so excited about him signing the book that I didn't realize until after he left that he had misspelled my name as "Kieth Wilson." It was the same situation as when Jet magazine misspelled my sister's name as "Vernesa" when she was featured in it. Mr. Kent died two years after he signed that book for me, but I still cherish that book today.

In the words of the song that Mr. Kent used to close his radio show with, he really "opened our eyes" and exposed his listeners to different types of music. Because he was willing to play a wide variety of music,

Mr. Kent had a historically long career in radio. He played house music, R&B, rock, soul, blues, Jazz and of course, steppers' music. His female on-air sidekicks, along with his many fans, called him "Herbie Baby!"

I have never really thought that there was a career that I couldn't pursue, because I felt like I had been studying and preparing all my life for many professional options. My parents always gave me opportunities to reach my potential throughout my life. They were always killing themselves to make sure their children accessed all of their individual talent and potential.

My parents are both avid readers who encouraged us and made sure that we all read as much as possible. My teachers in Catholic school were impressed with my vocabulary and use of language when I transferred to Saints Peter and Paul. I have always wanted to learn and be challenged by new things, because you never know where you might land in life.

Thanks to my parents, I was an avid reader and loved books, especially those dealing with history and science. Once I was safely able to study in my new Catholic school, I could really thrive. I really wanted to learn more than what was being taught at school. In the early 1970s, encyclopedias were becoming something that most homes with kids were encouraged to purchase, but they were very expensive. However, more and more homes had in-home libraries so their children could read what they wanted about the world in the privacy of their own homes.

During the second season of *Good Times*, they aired an episode titled "The Encyclopedia Hustle." It begins with "Little Michael" talking to his mom about how he wants to learn more about Black history. While they are talking, there is a knock at the door, and in walks actor Ron Glass portraying a supposedly blind encyclopedia salesman.

On its surface, the premise of the encyclopedia plot of a blind encyclopedia salesman in the projects was completely ridiculous, but the writers of the episode couldn't be knocked for lack of imagination .The episode ends with the salesman giving the Evans family a refund on the overpriced books. Some people believed that my dad owned a yacht while we lived in the projects, so anything is possible. Selling encyclopedias and installing plastic covers on furniture were two lucrative hustles in the 1970s. Every inch of a cloth portion of furniture in the living room would be meticulously covered with precisely measured plastic.

In the '70s, long before home computers and Google, families with young children were being encouraged to build home libraries featuring these bound books of information. World Book, The Book of Knowledge and Britannica were some of the best-known brands. In most cases, each letter had its own book. Even local grocery stores like Jewel Foods were selling encyclopedias. They sold one letter (book) every couple of weeks, which was a good marketing plan to keep loyal customers coming through their doors.

Those hardcover books had wonderful pictures and stories, and they were coveted by students who wanted to be successful in their studies. When you were doing a report on Greek mythology, that volume with the letter G had all the necessary information. Those expensive-looking books were kept on special bookshelves or glass cases in the home and were to be touched for serious viewing only.

One day, this young White guy rang our doorbell on South Jeffery. Dad really was not in any mood for his sales pitch, but this sales guy was good. He spoke in the language of how he could help educate young kids. "These books could help your kids get ahead," the salesman insisted. He spoke about how these kinds of books could really help kids compete in the world, which appealed to my parents immediately.

The young salesman pulled out a couple of volumes and showed the books to us. In the books were pictures of rockets, which I loved, along with pictures of U.S. maps. My sisters and I pleaded with our dad to invest in the books. We told him how we would get good grades and study hard. My dad, the tough Marine, turned to my mother, who likely said, "James, it's worth it." Just like on the show, my dad signed a contract with many small payments.

I was so excited about the encyclopedias that would soon arrive to our home. My cousins Tammy and Cedric in Tennessee both had

World Books Encyclopedias. In our order, we even got a free Black history book like that free Black calendar Ron Glass's character gave the Evans family when they placed their order.

In the Wilson home, it was a sin to mess up anything that our parents paid a lot of money for. Two things that were valued in our household were our living room furniture and our encyclopedias. Sitting on that plastic-covered living room couch when company wasn't present or spilling pop on an encyclopedia could result in punishment.

For me, these encyclopedias provided an escape and a place to design dreams. These beautifully designed and researched books became the basis of future stories and actually made me feel smarter. Using those books made me see the world as limitless and full of potential. I loved those books, and I loved my parents more for buying them for us, because I knew it was another costly sacrifice they made so we could reach our full potential.

When my dad signed that contract with the 48 easy payments, he was so proud to bring a tool to help his kids succeed. He bought a special bookcase for the encyclopedias, too. I remember like it was yesterday when the White salesman dropped off the big boxes at our home. I could tell that the salesman was a real hustler because he was able to talk my dad, who was very frugal, into making a major purchase. That was March 1, 1972, and we still have those encyclopedias to this day.

Even with the 48 low payments, the cost of the books was very expensive in the long run. It was probably an "easy credit rip-off." But my parents still signed on the dotted line anyway. I knew my mother and father were not able to pay for the whole set of encyclopedias up front, so they did what they had to do. Even with the long credit terms, it was worth it. It was an investment in our future.

"NOT GETTING HASSLED, NOT GETTING HUSTLED!"

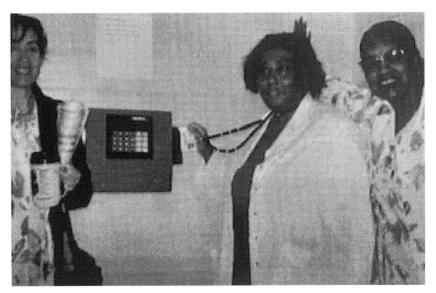

Mom punching out at Mercy Hospital
Bronzeville, Chicago 60616

CHAPTER 7
"Black Jesus"
Originally aired February 15, 1974

In the episode titled "Black Jesus," Little Michael is very proud of one piece of art that J.J. has created. In the episode, J.J. painted a picture of Jesus using the likeness of Ned, the neighborhood wino. By the time this episode was on the air, I was deeply immersed in Catholic school education at Saints Peter and Paul School in South Chicago. By the end of my third-grade year, I had been bombarded with pictures, rosaries and crucifixes with the very familiar "White" Jesus. The illustrations were always of a White guy with wavy hair and blue eyes.

While I enjoyed my Catholic education, I also developed a very inquisitive personality, and I had a tendency to question everything, like Michael on *Good Times*. Using the encyclopedias my parents purchased for the family, I researched the questions I had about the world.

When you attend Catholic school, you see images of Jesus all day with blue eyes and white skin. Eventually, you tend to take what you see for granted. The images around you in the schools, churches and books make you believe that Jesus is White in real life. I never thought much about Jesus' ethnic origins until I started reading my encyclopedias and seeing pictures of Middle Eastern people in the *National Geographic* magazines Dad brought home. I also questioned how Jesus might have looked when I saw educational television programs on WTTW Channel 11, our local PBS affiliate. I was only in about the fifth or sixth grade at that time, but I learned to question everything.

The images in those magazines were different from the ones on the walls of my school and church. In addition to our encyclopedias, I also loved reading *Popular Mechanics, Look and Reader's Digest* magazines. But the magazine that most intrigued me was *National Geographic*. It could have been the topless ladies I saw on the pages, but I really can't say.

At an early age, a lot of incoming scientific data and religious imagery was impacting my developing world view. Because of the daily bombardment of the fair-skinned religious images I saw at school, I was awestruck when I saw the *Good Times* episode featuring a Black Jesus. I was really blown away when I heard Michael quote the biblical description of Jesus that he found in the book of Revelation: "hair like wool and eyes of fire." I had *never* heard that description of Jesus until that *Good Times* episode.

It then became very plausible to me that Jesus could have been a Black man. I actually was unfamiliar with that passage, so I had to check it out in my favorite Bible, which ironically had the stereotypical blue-eyed Jesus inside it. This "revelation" was one of the most impactful in my life. Everything changed from that point.

I remember enjoying the Black Jesus episode and how James Evans viewed the Black Jesus picture as a good luck charm. This was contradictory to me, because by this stage in life, I had spent a lot of time in church, and people usually talked in terms of having faith, not luck. What did they say in church down South? "Trust in the unchanging hand of Jesus!"

In terms of Christian faith, Mom and Dad were Baptist at that time, but I was attending Catholic mass at school during the week and most Sundays. In all honesty, my religious experience was the most intense when my sisters and I went south to Nashville in the summers. Church down there was loud and long!

There was no such thing as a Black Catholic in Nashville in my family. Most Christians in Nashville were Evangelical Christian, usually Baptist, African Methodist Episcopal, Methodist or Seventh Day Adventist. Nashville is the place where I first heard the terms "sanctified" and "saved." It was in the Bible Belt, where alcohol wasn't sold until later in the day on Sundays. TV stations went off the air at midnight or 1 a.m. at the latest. Religious-themed shows were on television and the radio *all* day on Sundays back then. Clearly, escaping Jesus was impossible.

Ministers in the South were often Reverend Ike types. Reverend Frederick J. Eikerenkoetter II, better known as Reverend Ike, was a popular Black Evangelist often seen and heard on television and radio during that time. I used to call him the "hollerin'" preacher! He looked like a walking billboard for a Cadillac commercial, with his colorful suits. He had his classic foot stomping and "HWAH" at the end of each phrase. He was almost like James Brown with his persona and delivery style.

Like Reverend Ike, many ministers in Nashville wore flashy clothes and did the obligatory screaming when they preached the "fire and brimstone" sermons. My Grandma Otie B's second husband, Reverend Smith, reminded me of Reverend Ike. In my eight-year-old mind, I was sure they all drove fancy Cadillacs. During church services, there was always that coordinated call and response with the organist. There was often some speaking in tongues too. Somebody had to fall out at least once during the long service. Then one of the ladies in the nurse outfits would come over with a fan and a glass of water to render aid. We didn't do all that at the Catholic church.

Back at home in Chicago, we were never far from my parents' Tennessee roots. My Dad was a fan of Charley Pride songs, Tennessee Pride sausages and, of course, *Hee Haw* on television. "Where, where are you tonight? I searched the world over and thought it was true love, you found another and 'pfftt' you were gone!" I just can't forget that song. *Hee Haw* was actually a pretty good show. Minnie Pearl was funny, and Roy Clark could play that guitar. There weren't a lot of brothers on that show, though.

Church was never far from our home; it was as close as the living room television set. Mom would watch Reverend Billy Graham, who was big on both television and radio. Reverend Graham touched people of all races with his message. He would interact with presidents from Eisenhower to Trump, and he died in 2018 at age 99. From 1943 to

1944, Reverend Graham was briefly a minister at First Baptist Church in Western Springs, Illinois, just west of Chicago. By the 1950s and 1960s, Reverend Graham would become known for his Billy Graham Crusades. During his Crusades, he would appear at large stadiums across the country where fans would shout out his name. Down South, Graham was really big. He impacted churches all throughout the Bible Belt.

My parents both love Nashville and called it their hometown, though technically Mom was born in Fayetteville, Tennessee, a small town located about 40 miles south of Nashville. It's like people from Kankakee saying they are from Chicago.

Mom moved to Nashville with her mother after graduating from Fayetteville High School. My mom was a member of the Owens clan, who were the children of Roberta and Collier (Carl) Owens Sr. The couple had 13 children and operated a cotton farm in Fayetteville. Nashville became the Owens family home after my grandfather died. When Grandmother Roberta became a widow, she still had a number of her 13 children living with her, including my mother, so she moved with them to the capital of Tennessee to find work.

My Grandma Otie B. Smith was born in Nashville. Her first husband, Taylor, was my dad's father, which is why my dad's middle name is Taylor. I never knew either of my grandfathers. Grandma Otie B. would later remarry to Reverend Smith, whom she also outlived. She resided in Nashville until she passed away at age 103.

My parents wanted to make sure we experienced Nashville, so my sisters and I were sent there at the end of the school year throughout our youth. It was an opportunity to spend the summer with our relatives and connect with our "Southern Cousins." Our Nashville summers were filled with Saturday and Sunday worship because of our two religious grandmothers who both lived in Nashville. Church attendance was very important to both of them. My Grandmother Roberta Owens was a Seventh-day Adventist who took us to Hillcrest Seventh-day Adventist Church on Saturdays, and my Grandmother Otie B. Smith was Baptist, so we went to church on Sundays with her.

Summer weekends in Nashville were filled with church because of their varying denominations.

Down South, church services went on for hours, which was torture for a kid who was used to timing his Sunday social agenda by the predictable ending time of the one-hour mass at Saints Peter and Paul School. After 9 a.m. mass in Chicago, we returned home in time to see *The Cisco Kid* and *The Lone Ranger* on Channel 9 with the commercials from Bert Weinman Ford located at 3535 N. Ashland Avenue. (Those commercials never worked on my dad because he always got his Fords from Burt Rose Ford in Roseland.) But down South, the first hour was just the warm up!

By the time summer ended and we were heading back to Chicago, I was feeling churched out. I know that sounds bad, but I was only about eight years old and I had not ever spent that much time in church at home. Once home, there would be no more being driven crazy by all the church ladies waving fans with a picture of Jesus on one side and the address of some funeral home on the other. I remember the giant pictures of Jesus in the sanctuary with the outstretched hands that hung over the baptismal area.

I still LOVED my summers in that town! My cousins and I had great times! But I was totally fine going back to Catholic church when I returned home. No more whooping and hollering! No more folks speaking in tongues. No more endless songs. Down South, I would be in church for what seemed like hours hearing about the goodness of this man named Jesus. The organist and priest in Catholic church didn't have that cat and mouse thing going on like down South. This city Catholic boy was in hell down there.

Those kinds of thoughts would have gotten me kicked out of the family. I certainly couldn't talk that crap around either of my grandmothers. The seven-year-old me seemed to be having a "revelation" that White Jesus was causing me all this hell. As I sat in those Southern churches, my mind would wander all the time. "What is wrong with me? There goes that organ! Cue the tambourine, Jesus on the mainline. Thank God that it's the time where the Elders are calling the kids up for Vacation Bible School. We are outta here!"

My cousins and I would then sneak off to the neighboring Ben Franklin Drug Store for some candy. I remember it being so hot running over that parking lot. They had some good candy for a fat boy. I loved the apple bubble gum they sold there. My cousin Lamon Buchanan is a minister now.

My Grandma Roberta could remember all of the names of her multitudes of grandchildren and great-grandchildren. She had bookcases in her living room with pictures of each one of us. Making Grandma Roberta's wall of fame with pictures from big moments like weddings and graduations was big. Grandma could grow some flowers and cook some food! When she spoke, she had a high-pitched voice that sounded like Julia Child. She was such a sweet lady. Her apartment was located off Buena Vista Pike and always had big flowers that she planted in front of it. She did have a slight roach problem, just like we did in the projects.

Grandma Roberta also had a little dog named Tudor that looked like Petey on *The Little Rascals*. When she would call him, it would sound like she said "TOODAH!" My favorite picture of her is of her riding on a bus for work. In the picture she looked like Rosa Parks. Grandma Roberta worked for about 30 years after her husband died. She became a well-respected elder at Hillcrest, where she attended until her 90s.

Those summer treks to Nashville were my parents' way of making sure that we knew our family's roots. I am eternally grateful for all of those summers with my Tennessee family because when my parents left Nashville, they left all of their family behind. Being disconnected from their roots was hard at times for my parents.

My Dad's cousin Sonny, like my family, also lived in public housing for a short time before purchasing his first home on 89th and Michigan, where he lived with his wife, Leslie, and three of his children: my cousins Cecil, Lolitha (Leetha) and Cynthia (Cynthee) Westmoreland. My cousin Leetha reminded me of Mary J. Blige when she was young.

Most of my parents' family members lived in Nashville with a couple of exceptions. Mom's sister Lorraine (Rene) Owens remained in Fayetteville after marrying my Uncle JD Parks and never lived in Nashville. Aunt Rene could really cook! As one of the oldest siblings,

Aunt Rene helped to raise my mom and some of the younger Owens children. She made sure that all of them completed high school, though she did not graduate herself.

My grandfather Collier's death was a turning point for Mom and her family. Mom recounted the story of how he died after a stroke on the family farm. He was working on his car and was found unresponsive. My aunts Mildred and Rene had to pick him up and place him in his car and rush him to the hospital. Mom said that neither of my aunts had driven a car before, but since my aunt Mildred knew how to drive a tractor, she was able to put the car (which had a manual transmission) in gear and drive him to the hospital. Their father was pronounced dead at the hospital. Mom believes that he likely had died before ever reaching the hospital.

I never got to know him, but my mom told me how Grandad "Carl" was a Mason and a good public speaker who could convince people to follow him to the ends of the earth with his winning personality. She told me that he was very popular, and she was sure that she had at least one "other" brother outside of the family. It also would seem that his genes were responsible for his male progeny inheriting his dissolving hairline. We all had so much hair as youth. Who knew? Thanks, Grandad!

Aunt Rene was my cousin Margaret (Sis) Parks's mother. Both she and her sister, Bea Parks, lived for a short time with my parents in Chicago after finishing college at Tennessee State. They were like many relatives who came to Chicago for job opportunities from Tennessee, but would move back to Nashville after experiencing one of our famous Chicago winters. Rene's daughter Valerie and my cousin Shana (Sis's daughter) would visit Chicago and stay with my family on a couple of occasions. Valerie and Shana are so close in age that they were raised like sisters throughout their lives. Both are also alumni of Tennessee State University (TSU), which is like my family's college. I have about 20 cousins who attended TSU.

My cousins Cedric and Linda (Faye) Lamb were like sister and brother after Faye moved in with my Uncle Ezell and Aunt Mildred. She is the brother to Danny Lamb, who stayed with my parents. Faye moved from Fayetteville to Nashville after her mother, Stella, died. She attended high school and Tennessee State while living with my aunt and uncle.

Dad's mother, my Grandmother Otie B, was a short, Baptist woman and a snazzy dresser. She loved her gospel music. When I used to visit her, she dipped snuff and would ask me to dump her snuff can. I hated that coffee can that she spit chewed snuff in. She was a long-term cook at one of Nashville's most famous soul food restaurants called Swett's.

As the oldest son, my dad was one of the main cooks for his family growing up and learned to cook some soul food. (Paula Deen made a lot of money cooking what Black people have been eating since the time of slavery, but I digress.) Dad was also a cook in the Marines. His family grew up on this Southern cuisine, so it was always an important part of our household when we were growing up. When we celebrated my Grandmother Otie's 100th birthday in 2015, we held part of the weekend's celebration at Swett's.

In her later years, Grandma Otie lived with my dad's younger sister, my Aunt Evelyn. We were very blessed to come together as a family for Grandma Otie B's 100th birthday in Evelyn's apartment. Folks who had not been together for years were singing "Happy Birthday" to this matron of our family. We even had a caramel cake from Angelica's Bakery, a bakery owned by my friend and neighbor Paul Stokes from back home.

Grandma Otie B didn't leave home anymore, so we also had a bigger celebration without her with other family members at Swett's Soul Food Diner, where she worked for many years. Swett's is now in a new location, larger than the one I used to visit in my youth. When I was a little guy, as soon as we pulled into town, Dad would take us to see his mother at the old Swett's Restaurant. As soon as we walked through the doors of that restaurant, there was Grandma Otie with her little apron and hair net. She would rush from behind the lunch counter and give us all a hug!

The son of the original restaurant owner was present on the day we celebrated Grandmother's birthday at the new restaurant, and he spoke to me about memories of my grandmother working at the original restaurant when he was growing up. The food was pretty good, but not as good as my dad's cooking.

Grandma Otie was then 100 years old, and I just can't help but believe that one reason she lived so long was that she was never shy about having a beer or two and a shot of something brown and liquid over her century of life. Grandma Otie was tough at times, but was a big-time lady of faith. She always had a big Bible on her coffee table in her living room when we grew up. In her youth she wore some really cool hats!

When we were trying to calculate her 100th birthdate, my sister Ramona had to check census records because she did not have a birth certificate. Like many Blacks born in her era, Grandma Otie was born outside of a hospital. My dad was born in a Nashville hospital, but for many years we celebrated his birthday on the wrong date because of confusion with his birth certificate. When applying for his Social Security benefits, Dad found out that he was actually born on New Year's Day in 1936, not New Year's Eve in 1935 as we had thought. He was born the same year as Jesse Owens's triumph at the infamous Olympic Games in Germany.

I am indebted to my Tennessee grandmothers, cousins, aunts and uncles for adding to my life through the impact they had on me when I visited with them in Nashville. When we were in Nashville, I often stayed with my Aunt Mildred Owens, who was married to my Uncle Ezell. Their only child, Cedric, was five years older than me, so sometimes I felt like Bobby Brady, the bratty little brother to Greg Brady, around him. Cedric was always the big brother type towards me when I stayed with his family. I rode on a motorcycle for the first time with him. It was a classic Honda that was so cool! (No helmets, though! Don't tell my mother!) I always had a great time with him!

Cedric, who played the clarinet, introduced me to the music of the group Chicago one day when he played one of their albums on a reel-to-reel. I lived in Chicago and had never listened to a song of theirs until that day my Nashville cousin played their music for me. Ironic! They are known for a great horn section, which might be why he was fond of them. Because of listening to songs like "Saturday in the Park," I grew to love their music. I love that group to this day, and I have seen them in concert with Earth, Wind & Fire, my all-time favorite group. Cedric has worked as a videographer with area musicians in Nashville. He has also worked with the a cappella gospel group Take 6, who are Seventh Day Adventist like him and my Grandmother Roberta.

When his dad, my Uncle Ezell, suffered kidney failure, Cedric gave his father one of his. This was such a human-interest story that it made the *Tennessean* newspaper. In a cruel twist when Cedric reached middle age, his remaining kidney failed and forced him on kidney dialysis three days a week. He, like many Black people, is now on the organ transplant waiting list for a new kidney.

During those southern summer stays, my sisters would usually stay with my mom's sister Betty Owens Jackson. She had three older daughters: Jaunifer (Jan) and Niecy, who were in high school, and Tammy, who was the same age as my sisters. Jan was in the same class as the future media queen Ms. Oprah Winfrey. Oprah's dad also owned a barber shop a couple of blocks from Grandma Otie B's house.

While my sisters were hanging in East Nashville with my cousin Tammy, I was getting to know my various male cousins. I got to know my mother's younger sister Esther's sons Pooh, Stinkah and "Mont," short for LaMon. I only recently learned their government names! She also had three older daughters, Priscilla, Theresa and Pam.

During one of those summer stays, my cousin Theresa braided my hair and had me looking like Leroy from *Fame*. Both boys and girls had their hair braided in Nashville in those days. When it was time to head back to the South Side of Chicago, I and pulled them out before I got back home. I wasn't sure how well they would go with my Catholic school uniform. As an adult, I have visited Jamaica a couple of times, where I would see young White girls getting their hair braided on the Jamaican shores. But you always saw them combing them out on the plane ride before returning to America and their corporate jobs. They like the culture when it's convenient. But again, I digress!

Our Tennessee cousins were like our siblings by the end of those summers. During the summers, we developed a bond that made it kind of hard to get in the car to leave. We really had some special times with our cousins in the red hills of Tennessee. We were always going to church during those summers, which brought all of my cousins, aunts and uncles together. I really can't separate family from faith because of that Southern experience.

During those car rides back to Chicago, I would often ponder life. My parents had a 1972 Red Pinto with no air conditioning. As we buzzed up Interstate 65 back to Chicago, it was a long ride. Mom and Dad were up front, and we three kids were packed in that back seat. I hated having my knees in the air while sitting in the middle over the transmission hump when it was my turn to "ride the hump."

Our Pinto made a buzzing sound as it chugged up the highway. Those hills were rough on that 4-cylinder engine. That car would eventually become my first car. We only had AM radio, and we were always clicking the buttons trying to find a radio station. During those trips, we listened to rock or country music through the car's speakers until we lucked up on a Black radio station or a station playing a Black song. On that ride home, I would hear songs by my new favorite group, Chicago. I also learned to like other rock groups like the Eagles and Queen.

As we reached Northern Kentucky or the bottom of Indiana, Chicago's WLS radio would finally come in strong enough that we could hear the signal on our AM radio. WLS was the most powerful and popular AM radio station in Chicago. Though mainly a rock format, WLS played a lot of Black artists too.

These long car rides gave me time to reflect on things, and I grew to love the long drives. As my mind would wander while I was looking out the window into cornfields and rolling hills, I started feeling like little Michael, because I was really gathering a lot of data supporting my developing view that Jesus was Black. I really don't know why my mind was drawing that conclusion, but I remember just going to bed one night and saying, "Jesus is Black!" He had to be a cool dude like my family in church!

When we returned home that summer, Mom really started having strong feelings about wanting to convert to Catholicism. I think she was really influenced by Catholic Haitian coworkers at Mercy that she became close to, like Marie Noisette. We also had Haitian friends and neighbors like the Hoseas, who lived the next street over on 90th and Euclid. The Hosea kids attended Saints Peter and Paul with us, along with the Beaudoins, another Haitian family. Appolon Beaudoin was one year ahead of me in my friend Cathy's class. When I initially tried to join my fraternity as an undergraduate, I made another great friend and current fraternity brother Walter Duval, who was also a Haitian Catholic.

During this time, we went to a variety of churches, including Bethany Lutheran, which was on the next block from our home on Jeffery. As students at Saints Peter and Paul, we were required to attend family mass, and we also visited St. Ailbe with the Bumpas family. It was during these years that our family's religious foundations were evolving and developing.

Mom's good friend Elvira was a very devout practicing Catholic and probably had the most influence on her developing religious views. Mom spent a lot of time with Elvira after she and her husband Walter (Big Walter) moved in three blocks away on Constance Avenue with their son Stephen (Stevie) and his older brother Walter Jr. (Little Walter). I would become good friends with Stevie, who was just a year younger than me.

In 1974 or 1975, Stevie's mother took me, him and another neighbor to a brand-new shopping center called River Oaks located in Calumet City, which is in the south suburbs of Chicago. We took Stony Island to the Calumet Expressway and headed south in their nice Cadillac Sedan de Ville. After what seemed like a long ride, we got off at 159th Street and headed east to Torrance Avenue. That car had some soft leather seats as I recall. I wonder if it was "Corinthian leather" like in a Cordoba? (Long before *Fantasy Island* and playing Khan on *Star Trek*, Ricardo Montalbán was the voice of the Chrysler "Core Doh Bah"! He could roll that tongue for that R.)

The first destination after that drive was a discount store called Venture. Venture was just to the east on 159th from Elizabeth Seton Catholic High School in neighboring South Holland, where my sisters would eventually attend high school. My sisters had to catch a long bus ride from 91st and Jeffery to reach this school. One of my sister Yvette's classmates named Kim, who eventually married my buddy Gerard, used to ride that same bus with her.

After shopping, we were going to Red Lobster in nearby Dolton on Sibley (147th) for an "All you can eat Popcorn Shrimp" meal. Once we finished shopping, we were surprised with the word "nigger" in catsup on the windshield of the Bumpases' Cadillac. Here we go again with that word! Mrs. Bumpas cleaned the windshield like nothing happened and we headed to Red Lobster.

When we reached Red Lobster, there was a very long line, so Stevie's mother took a number and we boys went into the parking lot to play catch at the back of the lot by a fence. Behind that fence were new homes that were being built. All of a sudden, some neighborhood White boys started throwing rocks at us. They called us "niggers," and they clearly wanted to fight us. After some words, we rejoined Stevie's mom inside the restaurant, where we all chowed down on shrimp! Priorities!

Throughout the 1980s and 1990s, Blacks were leaving Chicago and relocating to south suburban communities like Calumet City, South Holland, Markham, Matteson, Country Club Hills and Harvey. It soon became clear that Blacks who dared to live in these towns or even shop there would not encounter polite welcoming committees. Instead, Blacks often encountered hostility or even danger. Blacks who thought the suburbs were always safe would learn otherwise.

My mother became really active at Saints Peter and Paul School, and after a number of years of being on the fence, she decided that we would begin Catholic instruction as a family. My father didn't convert, but he still supported my mom's efforts. On April 14, 1974, my mother and her three children were all baptized into the Catholic faith. Though my dad never officially converted, he attended family mass with us every Sunday. Elvira Bumpas would be my mom's Catholic sponsor, and her older son Walter Jr. (Little Walter) would become mine.

In my early youth, I had only seen White priests and pictures of a White Jesus. That all changed one Sunday when my family attended mass with our friends at St. Ailbe. On that fateful Sunday morning, we sat in the pews in the sanctuary at St. Ailbe and heard something that I only heard those Sunday mornings in Nashville, but never experienced in a Catholic church. (What made it nice was that it was done in an hour.) From that pulpit, I heard the voice of a Black man in a Catholic church speaking like Martin Luther King Jr. and Malcom X. St. Ailbe had a new priest named Fr. John Calicott. This Black man, the first Black priest I had ever seen, was raised on the South Side of Chicago after his family migrated from Mississippi as part of the Great Migration.

Years later when I attended Holy Angels Church in Bronzeville, Fr. John Calicott would become the pastor there. My wife, Denise, and I are current members of that very church. Fr. Calicott and his siblings had grown up in the Ida B. Wells housing projects. That housing complex was named after a famous Bronzeville resident who was one of the founders of the NAACP. Ms. Wells was a graduate of Fisk University in Nashville, located near my father's high school. She was also a famous journalist and activist. In 2019, a street in downtown Chicago was renamed in her honor.

In the late 1800s, Fr. Augustus Tolton was the first African-American priest ordained in the United States. Fr. Tolton lived many years in the Bronzeville community, where he served the increasing Black population that was moving northward from the South to find work in the many factories of Chicago during the beginning of the Great Migration. There weren't many options for Black Catholics who were migrating north, so the Archdiocese of Chicago brought Fr. Tolton to that community to address this challenge. The Catholic Church, even in the North, was separate but equal during that time. The vibrant Black Catholic community in Chicago, which I am still a part of, exists today because of the many Blacks Fr. Tolton converted to Catholicism during his short life.

That Black Catholic history is currently being challenged as five Black Catholic churches with connections to Fr. Tolton were just consolidated at the Holy Angels site and is being renamed Our Lady of Africa on July,1st 2021. The newly combined church will include Corpus Christi, St. Anselm, St. Elizabeth, St. Ambrose and Holy Angels. This is making my affiliation with the Catholic church very challenged at this moment in time!

The Black Catholic church lost this great figure prematurely when Fr. Tolton began having "spells of illness" in 1893. Fr. Tolton then took a temporary leave of absence from his duties at St. Monica's Parish (currently St. Elizabeth) in 1895. At the age of 43, on July 9, 1897, Fr. Tolton died at Mercy Hospital as a result of a heat wave in Chicago.

Fr. Tolton is buried in the priests' lot in St. Peter's Cemetery in Quincy, Illinois. He is currently under the canonization process to become the first African-American male saint. He is the reason that being Black and Catholic in Chicago is seen as a normal thing amongst a community that traditionally was not Catholic.

I can't emphasize enough how important that moment for me was when I saw Fr. Calicott preaching with the style of the many Southern preachers I had seen in Nashville. His existence gave me comfort that the Catholic faith was indeed right for me. Also, I made the connection that my new faith could be connected to my culture, so Jesus could indeed be Black, or at least a person of color. Being a Black Catholic man is not always that easy in our community, but it has always felt right.

"THANK YOU, BLACK JESUS!"

Just lookin' out of the window

CHAPTER 8
"The Lunch Money Ripoff"

Originally aired March 18, 1975

I n the opening scene of the *Good Times* episode "The Lunch Money Ripoff," Little Michael Evans is seen coming home acting very agitated and nervous. Like all mothers, Florida Evans can tell that something is wrong with her baby boy. Finally, Michael admits to his family that he is being bullied at school. I knew that feeling!

Michael was that smart, ambitious and slightly nerdy little know-it-all who felt he could change the world. In my head, I could see the scenes not shown, starting with Michael walking through the halls of the school minding his own business with his books in hand when some random kid asks, "What's up with smart boy?" He probably tries to ignore Eddie the bully, but despite Michael's attempts to avoid conflict, Eddie gets his friends to block Michael's path and probably knocks his books to the ground. In typical bully style, they hit Michael a couple of times and take his lunch money. This explains Michael's expression as he slams the door in the opening scene of this episode, where he is obviously ashamed and feeling pretty bad.

As a bullied kid in public school, I knew this kid. But even at Saints Peter and Paul, I would soon be reminded as a fat kid that bullies are everywhere. At Saints Peter and Paul, I was perfectly happy keeping to myself, studying and getting good grades. I spent most of my time just turning in my homework and waiting for the Scholastic Book Fair to show up with the latest and greatest books. If you had $5, you were a king at that book fair! It was a great thing when those new Peanuts books came in. *Charlotte's Web and The Autobiography of Miss Jane Pittman* are here! I saved up enough money so I could buy all of them!

Teachers generally liked me because I was a polite kid and always raised my hand to answer questions with excitement. I loved knowing the answer and maybe showing off a little. Catholic kids were mostly nice and respectful, but there were exceptions. Bullies are everywhere! A bully might be that kid who just doesn't like you or is jealous because you had the cool Mead Organizer while they had the cheap paper folders. Sometimes a bully's target was the kid with glasses or the fat kid like me.

My new bully was another Black boy in my class whose name I don't remember. I do remember the mild taunting from that kid started off during recess. He would hit me with cracks like "fat boy" and "Mr. Husky" as a reference to my large size and the Sears jeans that I wore in those days.

Our recess occurred in what was almost a concrete fort on the concrete parking lot adjacent to the school. The east wall was the back of Woolworth's located at 91st and Commercial, and the west wall was the school. The south wall was a very tall wall of about 15 feet of concrete which went straight up to 91st Street because our play lot sat below street level. The north wall was a chain link fence with a gate from the alley where the back entrance from the school allowed us access to the lot.

The highlight at recess for the boys was dodgeball. The teachers didn't watch the boys that closely, so the "no hitting in the face" rule wasn't always enforced. My new bully used those unsupervised times to light me up with that ball! Other kids used to think that was so funny! I was pretty slow and big and a big target. My boy Arnold Mireles was in the same situation, so we both hated recess! We were both in the fat boy club, as they used to call it!

One day in class after getting 100% on a test, I happened to look over at my bully's desk and see a whole lot of red marks on his test. I inadvertently made eye contact with him after looking at his test. When the teacher wasn't looking, he walked over to my desk and whispered in my ear, "I am going to kick your fat butt after school!" That wasn't good! Getting hit with a rubber ball was one thing, but getting hit with a fist was a little different.

I started thinking to myself that I had not had to run from school since running from those White boys at Warren, but I was going to run today! Like Michael, I knew that I couldn't run forever, but on that day, I was getting out of there! I knew in my mind that I would have to eventually have to "meet him outside" after school, but not today!

During class that day, I took time to size him up, because I realized that I had never really looked him in the eyes before that day. When I finally looked him over, I realized he was actually shorter than me and very skinny. I was still scared of him, so running home after school was still the plan, because I had never fought another Black dude who I assumed could fight. I was used to mainly scrapping with two or three punk White boys who popped me a couple of times, took my lunch and left. It was never a fair fight, which was symbolic of racism in general.

I had developed no real fighting skills up into this point in my life, but I had taken many punches. I had received a number of what were referred to as "Pumpkin Heads," a.k.a. bumps on the head, during my two years of terror at Warren. By two o'clock, the word was on the street that a fight was going down after school. How these fights were announced through the school without teachers and the principal knowing remains a mystery to this day. Like Tootsie Pops, "the world will never know!"

I knew that crunch time was right after school, so I planned my escape. Instead of leaving through the main entrance on 91st and Commercial, I decided I would exit through the back door by the alley and run my fat butt home.

I usually walked home with another classmate, Kevin Smith, who lived three streets over from me, but for some reason it didn't happen that day. Kevin was a Black classmate who was actually nice to me, except when he called me Wilson Pickett. Another nice guy who lived near me on Chappell was Lerone Wilson.

As I watched the hands of the clock approach the end of the day, I had my getaway all planned, so when the bell rang, I was out of there! It was time for the getaway, and I hit the back door, but there he was! Damn! Plan A foiled! He had his crew and an audience of 15 or so, and I was so done.

So, it's Plan B, which was to fight! Here we go. Then the bully says, "Thought you were going to get away, fat boy!" In my head, the answer was clearly "yes." So, it was going down. I dropped my books and prepared to meet my maker like Nino Brown at the end of *New Jack City.*

Unlike at Warren, the other guys didn't help him fight, they just made a circle around us and watched. It began with dude doing his little Muhammad Ali's Rumble in the Jungle dance, and he started swinging at me. He hit me in the gut! I am sure that he thought he did some damage, but it was a weak punch. Weak punches really don't hurt fat boys, so I was more shocked than hurt. In a reflex, I balled up my chubby little fist and popped him real hard in his nose, and it started to bleed!

I was so pumped up that I hit him a couple more times until he pulled out a pencil and stuck it in my eye and ran off. He didn't do any damage, but he scratched my cornea a little. That pencil put a brown spot in the white of my left eye that has never gone away. I went home without mentioning the fight. I did not know how my father was going to react, and I didn't need that in my life.

The next day, there was a bit of a commotion at school and we both had to go to the principal's office. We both went to Sister Petronet's office and explained our sides of the story. I was such a "nice" kid who never had any other problems, so the principal let me go back to class after hearing my story. The other guy was a known troublemaker and she believed me, so she punished him alone. The funny thing is that I think I really messed up dude's nose, but after defending myself, I felt like I was freed! Thank God, because Dad would have murdered me!

"ANYTIME YOU'RE OUT FROM UNDER!"

CHAPTER 9
"The Big Move"
Originally aired September 26, 1976

A fter my seventh grade of grammar school, I transferred from Saints Peter and Paul for the eighth grade to St. Joseph, another neighborhood Catholic school located on 88th and Marquette in 1976. My new school was across the street from Bowen Public High School.

As I was starting my new school in the fall of 1976, a two-part episode called "The Big Move" aired on *Good Times*. On this episode, the Evans family was in the process of relocating to Mississippi. This episode was relatable to me because with my move to a new school, my life was changing in major ways.

The episode begins with the Evans family excitedly awaiting moving plans, as James has secured a new job in Mississippi. The first installment of this two-part episode ends in a very dramatic scene where the audience learns that James was tragically killed in a car accident. In this iconic episode, the news is received by telegram in the midst of what should have been a very festive going-away party, and it goes from a joyful party to a somber gathering.

John Amos had been written off the show because of a dispute he had with Norman Lear. This move upset many viewers of the show and changed the trajectory and storylines of the show, resulting in more of a focus on J.J. The death of James Evans is one of those iconic deaths of a fictional Black character that works Black people up. Cochise in *Cooley High* is another fictional character whose death tugs at the hearts of the Black people watching the film. Who can forget that screeching El passing over Preach and Cochise that drowned out Preach's screams for help as he clutched the dying "Chise"? Another iconic Black death was that of Cornbread in the movie *Cornbread, Earl and Me*, starring a young Larry Fishburne. "All he wanted was a soda!"

After Florida receives the news that her beloved James has died, she becomes very stoic and unemotional. Her reaction confuses and angers her children. The kids were facing the tragic death of their father and looked to their mother for comfort and understanding, while she responded in a very emotionless and non-caring manner.

The closest to death that the Evans kids had dealt with was in another episode, " A friend in Need" with the star basketball player who tried to commit suicide with some sleeping pills in that apartment, but his life would be saved! Part 2 of "The Big Move" ends with one of the most iconic scenes in television history when Florida finally breaks down after all the guests have left and shatters a punchbowl. In the closing scene with her clutched fists in the air towards heaven, she screams the unforgettable "Damn, damn, damn!" The children finally see their mother express her anger and sadness as they flock to her side while the closing credits roll. That show makes me think of the fancy punchbowl my family owned, like the one Florida smashed at the end of that famous episode.

It was around the time of this Good Times episode that the concept of death became a reality for me. It seemed that after we moved for a "better" life, my family experienced the loss of a lot of our family members in the '70s. My parents both came from large families, and many of their siblings began to pass away. During the '70s, many of my aunts and uncles seemed to be dying for a variety of reasons including strokes, cancer, car accidents and even murder. We would have that increasingly familiar pattern of my parents receiving "the call," followed by the car ride to Nashville, the sad funeral, the repast, then the trip back home back to Chicago.

When you are a preteen, death feels like a foreign concept that only affects old people. But after a while, I started to recognize the pain of my parents as they grieved the loss of sisters, brothers and friends. I started to feel like the Evans kids at the end of that episode when their father died, because my parents were experiencing a tornado of death.

About then, I started to realize that death is something that actually hurts. On Star Trek, the guy wearing a red shirt in the landing party often died, but that was TV. A real aunt or uncle dying was another matter. My parents experienced a lot of pain when someone close to them died, which I really didn't get at the time.

My aunt Gloria Owens's funeral was one of the first that I remember. Aunt Gloria was my mom's youngest sibling. She was very beautiful and married to Alvin, a semi-famous gospel singer at the time. I met Aunt Gloria only one time in Youngstown, Ohio, during a family trip to Niagara Falls and Rochester, New York. Aunt Gloria was another family member who stayed with my parents in Englewood before I was born when she came to Chicago looking for work. She left when that first winter hit, like everyone else.

On that Rochester trip, we were going to see Dad's brother Bert Wilson and his wife Carole. His older sister Louise also lived there with my play uncle Rochester (they were never married). My dad's other sister, Dorothy Wilson Curry, lived there as well. Dorothy and Louise both stayed with my parents in Chicago for a while. My dad had five brothers and three sisters. Dad's youngest brother Tommie Wilson lived in Washington, D.C.

Dad's younger sister Evelyn Whitney, along with his brothers Anthony and Richard Wilson, still lived in Nashville during those years. Evelyn had three children: a daughter, Cheryl Smith (Dumpty), a son named Man and a younger daughter named Tonya. My aunt Evelyn unfortunately passed away a couple of years ago, leaving him with just his two siblings Richard and Dorothy still living. My dad did not escape a family nickname, as his mom called him "Brother."

As the oldest male in his family, Dad was often in charge when his father, Taylor Wilson, left their mother, which was one of the reasons my father joined the Marines at 17 to provide financial support to his family. The odd jobs he had just didn't bring enough money in to support the large family, so the military was a necessary maneuver.

At his sister Evelyn's funeral, Dad reunited with his old friend Junior, who used to work at a movie theater with him and his cousin Sonny. Junior was the older brother of his Nashville neighbor Hazel White. He and Junior would sometimes check out a movie for free when they worked at the theater. Those were the adventures of a poor Black man living in the South! Knowing my dad, I am sure that he made sure that he saw all the Western movies he loved.

During the 1970s and 1980s, we would lose so many family members from Nashville. My aunt Gloria's death was really shocking to my mom. Gloria was so pretty and so young when she died. Aunt Gloria's husband Alvin reminded me of Al Green because he looked like Mr. "Love and Happiness" with his cool suits. My only living memory of Aunt Gloria was at that stopover at her and Alvin's house in Ohio on the way to Rochester. It was the one and only time I would see my aunt Gloria alive.

About a year later, my grandmother Roberta was on the phone with the news that Aunt Gloria had died in a car accident. Mom cried at the news as Dad hugged her. My aunt Gloria and her husband Alvin were in a head-on collision while traveling in a VW Beetle on an Ohio expressway, and Aunt Gloria died instantly. Gloria's small daughters and husband survived the crash, though one daughter was smashed under a seat. Once Mom received the news of her sister Gloria's death, we were heading southbound on I-65 to Nashville for a funeral within a week. Aunt Gloria had moved to Ohio from Nashville, but she was laid to rest in her Tennessee hometown. After the funeral, the family gathered over my aunt Mildred's house for the repast.

Mildred Owens Thomison was another one of my mom's siblings and the unofficial Owens family coordinator. Mildred had the nickname "Grand" and was married to my uncle Ezell Thomison. Their house always had this uber-clean smell that I loved. Mildred had pretty hazel eyes. She was one of the aunts that I stayed with during summers in Nashville. Uncle Ezell used to remind me of Ron Isley.

My mom, Alease, also has an unusual family nickname of "Eechie." Nobody has ever explained that name to me. It sounds like a Grandma Roberta creation, much like how my uncle Collier (Carl Jr.) went by

June or June Bug, which I think was a play on how Grandma Roberta used to pronounce Junior. She would screech, "GUNE!" Grandma Roberta used to pronounce some words in a very unique way. Her voice sounded like a combination of Aunt Bee from *The Andy Griffith Show* and Julia Child.

Uncle Ezell loved iced tea and worked at Goodyear Tire in downtown Nashville. He really loved his job at Goodyear, and there was Goodyear everything throughout their house. Aunt Mildred and Uncle Ezell would host most of the family reunions and gatherings when we were growing up. Their home was in a very nice part of Nashville at 3131 Richmond Hill Drive. You would pass Old Hickory Lake before you reached the exit for their home at Brick Church Pike. We would also pass Grandma Roberta's church to get to Richmond Hill Drive.

When the family met up at Aunt Mildred's house after Aunt Gloria's funeral, it was just like when people met up in the Evans apartment after James Evans died. I can remember the women being in charge of making sure everyone had enough to eat and the cursory moments of sympathy with neighbors and church friends. Just like when James died, there was a slightly festive atmosphere mixed in with the sadness of his death.

On the wall at my aunt's house was a famous family portrait from the funeral for my aunt Stella, who had passed away in 1972 in Fayetteville, Tennessee, where my mother's family was raised. That family picture on that wall is etched in my mind as it has eight of the thirteen Owens siblings lined up in their finest clothing with a number of their children, including me, seated around them on the floor. I hated and loved that picture because it reminded me of one of the only times I was around most of my mother's sisters and brothers. There were so many people in the picture that you can only see half of my face in the lower corner of the picture. Every person I know in the family has a copy of that picture.

Grandma Roberta was very religious and named many of her children from characters in the Bible, which is why I have an aunt Esther Ruth (Esther) Owens. I also have uncles David, Moses, Paul and Sam. My grandmother Roberta also gave some of her children unusual names as well, like my mom's name Alease and her sister Adrue Kertcheval. They are two of the Owens siblings who look the most alike.

One of Adrue's daughters, Annie, also stayed with my parents for a while. Adrue had three other daughters, Barbara Joe (Bobbi Joe), Sheila and Wanda Kertcheval. I also have an uncle Collier (Carl Jr. aka June) and aunts Lorraine (Rene) Owens Parks, Gloria Owens McCottry and Stella Mae (Stella) Owens Lamb. There were also aunts Betty (Bet) Owens Jackson and Mildred (Grand) Owens Thomison with the pretty eyes.

At my parents' 60th anniversary, my dad's cousin Sonny once again served as witness for their vow renewal, just like he did in a Nashville courthouse 60 years earlier. Hazel White, his old neighbor from Nashville, was also there with her daughter Dana. My buddy Arnold Mireles's dad José and Arnold's brother Jaime attended with his sister Sonia. My childhood friends Cathy, Gerard and Kim were there as well. Many friends and family from near and far celebrated with us that day. My sisters and I did it big for our parents. We had many of the people who were a part of our lives present to celebrate our parents because we were so proud of them!

When we sought out something blue for my mother, my wife reupholstered a bench from a dining room set my parents purchased for their first home on Jeffery with a beautiful blue floral pattern to be used at the ceremony. They were so shocked when we pointed out the family heirloom that they were sitting on during their vow renewal.

One of the biggest surprises was when my cousin Danny showed up to celebrate with them. Danny was that surrogate child who lived with my parents all those years ago before their own children were born. They had not seen Danny for 30 years, and it really meant a lot to them to see him.

Death was constant for my parents in the 1970s and 1980s. The deaths on my father's side, ironically, were the main opportunities for me to connect with the Wilson side of my heritage because of strained relationships on my dad's side. My uncle Tommie Wilson in particular is a relative I didn't even have a personal recollection of because I spent such a very small time with him growing up. There is a picture of my family including Aunt Dorothy and Louise when we travelled to Washington, D.C., to see my uncle Tommie Wilson on the lawn of the U.S. Capitol Building. I am so young in that picture, which is the only memory I have with Uncle Tommie.

My uncle Anthony Wilson was murdered during that time, and I remember driving to Nashville and meeting up at my Grandmother Otie B's house before his funeral. Uncle Anthony had made some unfortunate choices in his life and was murdered as a result of them.

My dad really stressed to his children the importance of being honest and staying on the right side of the law, even though the law can be unfair to Black people. He told me a story about a time when he was working at the Morrison Hotel and money came up missing from a room. Dad was accused of stealing it because as a housekeeper, he had keys to all of the rooms. He even had to take a lie detector test to prove his innocence, which was humiliating. He believed that the law was often used unfairly against Black people.

My dad once took me out to a Tennessee prison to visit one of his brothers when I was about 10 years old. I remember the locking doors after being buzzed in and the glass partition. My dad gave my uncle some cartons of cigarettes and they talked a while. On the ride to meet back up with the rest of the family, he told me that he really cared about his brother but some bad choices had cost him. He told me to try to remember to make good choices. He didn't bring Mom or my sisters to that prison visit. That lesson was for me and me alone. I remember that prison visit with Dad and my uncle like it was yesterday. My dad wanted to discourage me from doing something that could get me in that situation. He wasn't judging his brother, just his choices.

Another reason that my dad joined the military when he was so young is that he knew that a life in Nashville might not end well for him. There were a lot of things that poor Black people ended up doing in the ghetto, and he wanted out! I know that it was hard for him to leave his family, but he wanted a better life.

Once, when I was in grammar school, we went to a police station just west of King Drive on 25th Street. We were going there to meet Officer Friendly. Officer Friendly was a program of volunteer police officers who were selected to improve the relationships and perceptions of police officers with young people. The station was about a block from our apartment. The irony is, they had us pretend to be locked up in that cell, and I knew I didn't like that idea after visiting a real prison. My younger sister Ramona is a long-time veteran officer of the Chicago Police Department. I have to think that my father's influence had a role in her career choice.

Those funerals also gave me a window into my dad's view of death. I remember when Grandma Otie called to tell him that his brother Bert was dying from cancer. My stoic dad was pretty upset! Though he didn't always show emotion, I knew he was sad. When Uncle Bert was buried back in his hometown of Nashville, there were some awkward exchanges because of tattered relationships with his siblings, but they all came together.

While I was in high school, my mom's friend Elvira was diagnosed with breast cancer. Ironically, her husband Walter was a big smoker, but it was the nonsmoking Elvira who was diagnosed with a cancer. It was so unfair! My boy Stevie took it really hard. His mom was so beautiful. She was here, then one day she was gone. Her death was really hard because in those days, I spent as much time with her as my real family.

Minnie Riperton, a very famous soul singer from Chicago, became the spokesperson for the American Cancer Society around the same time because she also was diagnosed with breast cancer. Her song "Lovin' You" makes me think about Stevie's mom. Minnie Riperton grew up on Oakwood Boulevard across the street from Holy Angels Church.

This period was so stressful and, in many ways, prepared me and my second wife, Denise, for one of the most difficult periods that we have had to deal with since marrying. Denise's mom, Juanita, passed away a couple of years ago after an extended illness. Though we knew her death was coming, we were still unprepared.

Before her mom died months earlier, Denise received a call at 1 a.m. from her brother Bob telling her that their mother had coded at home. We had experienced many near-death hospital experiences with Mom over the previous 10 years, but this time was different. When the ambulance took her to the hospital this time, she was unconscious. Mom would be in a coma for more than a month with her two children by her side, and it was unclear if they would ever speak to her again.

After a month of being in the hospital, Denise's mother passed away with her firstborn at her side. Denise was a doctor, but the person lying in the bed was her mother who was taking her rest in heaven that night. That was the toughest thing we have ever dealt with as couple. It was the absolute worst!

As her husband, I wished that I could take away Denise's pain, but I couldn't. I knew it was going to be hard for Denise, as she spoke to her mom almost every day. The woman who gave her life was now a soul at our Lord's side.

"MAN OH MANISCHEWITZ!"

Just lookin' out of the window

CHAPTER 10
"The Check Up"
Originally aired May 3, 1974

The episode "The Checkup" really sticks out in my mind because James Evans reminded me so much of my own father, James Wilson. In this episode, the hard-working James Evans was becoming increasingly irritable to family members and, like most Black men, refused to tell even his wife that something was bothering him. He was very short tempered during the episode and had no patience for any "mess," just like my dad.

What was so interesting about the episode was how Michael diagnosed his father as having hypertension from a description of the condition in a medical book he read. That is so much like something I would have done. I would have been checking out our Book of Knowledge encyclopedias or trying to see if *Ebony* had an article on the topic, which they often did.

Ebony and *Jet* magazines often had useful health and wellness articles featuring authors like Dr. Terry Mason, the first Black Chief Urologist hired at Mercy Hospital. Dr. Mason used to also do health segments on WVON and was often a lecturer at Project Alpha, where he spoke to young Black males about sexually transmitted diseases. Project Alpha is a National Program of Alpha Phi Alpha created by my home chapter, the Iota Delta Lambda Alumni Chapter of Chicago.

The "Checkup" episode went through the trials and tribulations of trying to convince this tough father to go the doctor for a checkup. This is not an uncommon problem in the Black community. Black people often cite the Tuskegee Experiment as a rationale for not going to the doctor. This is a reference to a medical experiment where Blacks were exposed to syphilis simply to see what would happen. This occurred between 1933 and 1972, ending just two years before *Good Times* premiered as a series.

In another classic moment in the episode, James very angrily smashes a chair against the wall and retreats to the bedroom, as he was unwilling to hear the appeals of his family to get checked out. After some discussion with his family members, led by the youngest member, "Little Michael," the family was finally able to get James to go the doctor.

In the "Checkup" episode, writers made sure that the doctor was portrayed by an African-American. This Black doctor would assure James that he did not have hypertension, but James did have high cholesterol, which both my dad and I suffer from as a result of poor eating habits.

The wonderfulness of this episode is how it addressed a true health concern that many African-Americans are afflicted by in a very believable manner. The writers highlighted how healthcare is a family dynamic in the Black community. Black people have real fears about going to the doctor stemming from real bad experiences in healthcare, which is at the root of our lack of trust in doctors.

The White doctor James Marion Sims is regarded as the father of modern OB/Gynecology. He was known to have cruelly experimented on many Black slave women without anesthesia so he could develop techniques in that field of medicine. I am always reminded that my good friend Cathy and my wife's cousin Dr. Renee' Ewing-Davis are both Black OB/Gynecologists who are living counterbalances to that hurtful legacy. Cathy is an OB physician who practiced at St. Bernard Hospital in Englewood. Our old principal from Saints Peter and Paul, Fr. McNamara, began his career there as a hospital chaplain. That just further illustrates how life is very circular. Renee' did her OB residency at Mercy when Mom worked there, and she actually met her long before I met my future wife, Denise. She also worked with Dr. Terry Mason while she was in residency at Mercy.

In 1973 or 1974, my dad began complaining about a pain in his stomach. At the time, our family diet included all of the staples of Black life with all kinds of fatty, salty, fried foods. Aside from being a mailman, dad was a serious cook. He often fried up country hams that we picked up during our trips to Nashville. Dad was G. Garvin long before that young TV chef was born. Dad fried many of our meals including chicken, pork chops and his specialty of hot water cornbread. He also made pinto beans, black beans and greens with a lot of salt content. Dad also loves to bake, and his specialties include pound cakes, chess pies and peach cobbler. He made hamburgers and hot dogs from time to time for us kids as well.

Those hamburgers were like the famous ghetto burgers Eddie Murphy talked about in his comedy show *Delirious*. Dad would fry up well-seasoned, thick, round beef patties, then place the tasty, greasy burgers on a plate covered with a paper towel to soak up any juices from them. After the burgers were done, Dad allowed us to take our pick of which ones we wanted to eat. That was one of the few times that we could choose what we wanted to eat!

Dad would often purchase a head of iceberg lettuce for a dime from the Jewel-Osco grocery store on 87th and Stony for the burgers. We had to unwrap the head of lettuce from Saran wrap, carefully tear off one leaf for a burger, then wrap it back up. You had to secure that lettuce tightly or it would turn brown before you could use it the next day. Letting lettuce go bad because you didn't rewrap it correctly was a bad look in the Wilson household!

We also put a carefully sliced piece of cheese on the burger. Dad would often bring blocks of government cheese home from his route because people often gifted them or food stamps to him at Christmas. Those blocks of "gubment" cheese made some great grilled cheese sandwiches back in the day. We would place that cheese between two pieces of white bread, usually Jewel brand or Wonder Bread, add catsup and mustard, then go to town. My dad used a well-seasoned cast iron skillet for cooking these masterpieces.

In the Wilson home, we also had Spam sandwiches, and my dad and I would eat sardines with mustard on crackers. Oscar Mayer bologna was also fried up and placed on bread. My cousin Shana's father, Bill Ward, worked many years for Oscar Mayer. We also ate hog head cheese on crackers.

For breakfast, Dad made pancakes and scrambled eggs with real bacon from Tennessee. We kids drank a lot of different flavors of Kool-Aid because a packet of it cost only five cents in those days. Add some sugar and water and you could make a whole pitcher of Kool-Aid with only one packet. We drank Yummy brand soda from Jewel-Osco. They came in ten flavors and were a dime per can. We ate pretty well, but maybe not all that healthy. Dad fried food in Crisco lard and stored the used fried grease in Folgers coffee cans, separating the fish grease from the chicken grease. That very diet that Michael described in that episode as being bad for Black folks was *our* diet. Every day, Dad was using citrate of magnesia, baking soda and Pepto Bismol, but his stomach kept acting up.

One day after work, Dad asked Mom to take him to the doctor. This was big, because my dad NEVER wanted to go to the doctor! He must have been feeling pretty bad. Mom loaded up the Ford Galaxie 500 and we were off to the University of Chicago Billings Hospital. We went to the emergency room, and the next thing I remember is "We are taking him to surgery now!" My dad had a ruptured and bleeding ulcer!

That news was really frightening for the whole family. My mother took us kids home and we stayed with our neighbors the Buckners, while Mom went back to stay at the hospital with Dad. The next day, after Dad was in a regular hospital room, Mom went back to the hospital with her good friend Elvira. They parked our family car on the "Midway" (short for the Midway Plaisance) near the hospital and walked in. Knowing my mother, I am sure that she had a care package for him with some new pajamas, his razors, some Irish Spring soap (his favorite), a *Chicago Defender,* a *Chicago Sun-Times* and a *Jet* magazine.

I would become very familiar with that hospital because I would work there from my junior year in high school through college with my buddy Gerard, who is now a registered nurse at that same hospital, having worked there for nearly 30 years. My niece Alyssa is now a registered nurse there as well, thanks to this same friend who hired her.

When that visit was over, Mom and her friend reached their parking spot, but they didn't see the car. They figured that they must have returned to the wrong spot, so they began to walk around looking for the car. Then it hit them. The car had been stolen! They had to call the police, report the theft and, worse yet, tell the man with a recently treated ulcer that the family car was just stolen!

If that wasn't enough, later that same year my sister Vanessa suddenly took ill. She was in the fifth or sixth grade and having a lot of constipation and stomach pain. Mom knew something wasn't right. One day the pain was so unbearable that Mom took my sister to Wyler Children Hospital, which was also a part of the University of Chicago hospital system. After an x-ray, they told Mom that my sister had an obstructed bowel and could die if she didn't have an emergency colostomy. Once again, Mom was at the University of Chicago Hospital because someone needed an emergency surgery.

They did the emergency procedure and saved my sister's life. Because of the surgery, she had to have a colostomy bag for a while when she was in grammar school. Vanessa now had something in addition to her blue and brown eyes and deafness in one ear to contend with at school. She and my mom were troopers during that time. For nearly a year, my sister had a colostomy bag until her bowel was eventually resected. That was tough for a young girl. My mom's friend Mrs. Karen Fields and her daughters were big supporters of my sister during that time.

St. Joseph was closing, so my sisters were also once again transferring to new schools for the third time after leaving Warren Public School. My sisters met the Fields girls at St. Joseph, where we

115

attended for one year. The next school they all transferred to was Immaculate Conception at 88th and Commercial Avenue. The Fields family was a constant part of our lives during those years. The oldest daughter, Laura Fields, and my sisters even became cheerleaders at their new grammar school. New adventures were starting!

"MY NAME IS LENNY AND IF YOU CAN'T GET IT HERE THEN THERE CAN'T BE THAT MANY!"

CHAPTER 11
"The Man I Most Admire"
Originally aired October 8, 1974

Good Times was the one of the first shows in television history to portray the image of a Black father who was married and living with his wife and kids. There were no children from other women! *Good Times* allowed America to see a typical Black family. This imagery was so needed, as the 1970s were probably one of the last eras in which the nuclear family was still a majority of most families of all races. It was the last generation of "fireplace" television viewing. This was when the family gathered around the one television and watched shows together. Things would change as more couples would divorce or just not marry at all in ensuing generations.

In the episode "The Man I Most Admire," my spiritual doppelganger Michael is pondering about many historical characters for an essay he was writing on that topic for school. Michael was torn about who to choose, considering Reverend Jesse Jackson Sr. among others. As Michael starts to ponder about the characteristics of this theoretical person, he comes to the realization that he needs to look no further than his father James.

By the fifth grade, I had become quite a studious kid with a thirst for knowledge about Black history. My parents were given a bonus history book titled *In Black America* when they purchased our family encyclopedias a few years earlier. I took a particular interest in that book because of its focus on Black history.

I was fascinated by the historical accounts of Black figures like Nat Turner, Crispus Attucks, Dr. Martin Luther King Jr. and Malcolm X. Even fictional accounts of history like *The Autobiography of Miss Jane Pittman* caught my interest because they were period pieces loosely based on historical events. I always watched the television version of the book staring Cicely Tyson that came on each year.

I would always have a silly recollection of Cicely Tyson portraying Miss Pittman drinking from the water fountain in a climactic scene. It is a silly inside joke, but I would be like, "I wouldn't want to drink behind that old slobbering lady either!" I know that is not cool, but it still makes me laugh! I just saw a beautiful picture of a 90-something Cicely Tyson posing with 47-year-old Regina King at the Golden Globes awards. They are two stunning representations of Black beauty and examples that "Black don't crack!" Ms Tyson now resides with the ancestors.

As a young man, I had a steady diet of *Ebony* magazine and various books that I withdrew from one of the two libraries I frequented, which were the South Chicago Library or the Avalon Library. I was always looking for cool books on Black figures. If I saw a name in a book or an article that seemed interesting, I would look for multiple sources on that person. I still try to do that today, especially in the era of social media with unreliable sites and satire sites that sometimes seem credible but are not. There was a time before Snopes.com!

The South Chicago Library was across the street from the South Chicago YMCA, where students from Saints Peter and Paul took gym because we did not have one in our school. Moose Cholak, a famous wrestler on Channel 32, used to work out at that Y. South Chicago Library was located on East 91st Street just past Commercial Avenue. It was also near Our Lady of Guadalupe Catholic Church, which held Spanish masses for the growing Mexican population of South Chicago.

The Avalon Library was on 88th and Stony Island next to my favorite Harold's Chicken Shack. That is where I first experienced the delightful taste of mild sauce on a quarter white of fried chicken. Both of these libraries were within walking distance of my home, with some effort. It was during those years that I developed my annoying habit of learning obscure facts. Odd things in history have always intrigued me.

Benjamin O. Davis Community Center on 91st and Jeffery was another place in my community where I would read and do research for book reports. Inside the lobby of that center was a picture of Benjamin O. Davis, the Black military hero who bears its name. There were times when I looked at the uniformed picture of General Davis at that center and thought the uniformed persona seemed familiar.

Every day I would see my dad iron his postal uniform with such pride in preparation for work the next day. He loved his uniform and often spoke of the fancy dress Marine uniform he wore when he served. Polishing shoes was an art form with him. My dad really emphasized making sure my uniform looked nice when I was a Cub Scout. As a former Marine, he had a keen idea of what a man in uniform was supposed to look like because of those many tough drill sergeants he had. My dad was a Marine who never learned how to swim, but still became a Marine. Oorah!

After September 11th 2001, I joined the Medical Division of the U.S. Army Reserves, where I wore a uniform like the ones Dad wore both in the Marines and as a United Postal worker. My younger sister, Ramona, has served as a Chicago police officer for over 25 years and also has put on a uniform like our dad!

When Dad was preparing his work uniform, he had a routine of covering the ironing board with a towel and a sheet, then carefully placing his shirts and pants on the ironing board. Dad would spray his shirts and pants with just the right amount of starch and make perfect creases. He would hang those items up the day before so he would never be late to work. Dad hates late people, and he always stressed to us that early is on time!

Every day around 4:30 a.m., Dad would make his coffee, prepare a little breakfast and head off to work. He would return home usually by 5:00 p.m., when we would see him emerge from our home's side door by the kitchen. Our home did not have a basement or garage, so

Dad parked his car in a small parking place in the alley right behind our house.

Parking on Jeffery was often illegal because it was a snow route in the winter and just reckless any other time. It was a boulevard and a bus route, which made parking on it very risky. One of my favorite cars, a Ford Escort GT, was totaled when I parked it in front of our house after a Jeffery Express bus took it out!

Dad was the main cook for the family, so after returning home and changing into his casual clothes, he would often prepare dinner. We generally ate dinner as a complete family, then proceeded to our various corners of the house. My sisters and I usually had some homework that we did at the kitchen table, while Mom did dishes or other housework.

By around seven o'clock, we often would meet up as a family to watch television in the living room. We would watch the shows like *Gomer Pyle* and *The Carol Burnett Show*. Of course, we didn't miss *Good Times!* We laughed at those shows together. My dad loves Westerns and would get mad when his favorite character died. Some of his favorite movies were The Good, The Bad and the Ugly and A *Fistful* of Dollars. Lee Marvin was his dude!

In good times and bad, we kids had a father providing wisdom and counsel. When we were making too much noise, we would hear the words "you know you better get that stuff together!" (The word "stuff" is the nice version of his order.) When we brought good grades home, there was praise and a special treat like French vanilla ice cream (his favorite). Bad grades did not get a good reaction. "I am paying all this money for that (blank) school and you bring home this? Turn off that television!"

My father was always dependable. On Mondays through Fridays and on holidays and weekends, Dad was there! In the rain, sleet or snow, he always delivered to his family. I used to get so angry about him saying things like "Act right!" or "Have some pride in yourself!" Or a favorite, "Get there on time!" Another one: "Is this the best you can do?" Or a command, "Get that hair cut!" Or, at least every week, "Cut that grass!"

One day after I was a college graduate, I realized that Dad was the man I most admired in my life. Indeed, I never had to look for some historic figure or sports star; I only needed to look to my kitchen table for my hero.

"Want Some Strap?"

My Dad in his postal uniform on his route in Englewood, Chicago 60621

CHAPTER 12
"The Mural"
Originally aired December 2, 1975

The essence of survival in the hood is having a crew or at least a best friend. Sometimes it is someone to fight your common enemy with, or the kid next door you trade baseball cards with. Though I was a very independent and self-sufficient kid, it was lonely on the battlefield. There were some days that I wished for a brother. There were also times I wished to fit in with the cool kids. Neither of those things happened for me.

When I first transferred to Saints Peter and Paul, I was feeling kind of lonely. On my first day in the third grade, the gentlest and kindest person I have ever met came into my life. It was 50 years ago, but I vividly remember meeting my first best friend. Like me, he didn't really fit in with the other budding athletes in our class or the popular kids in school. I was a new kid, and he was a Mexican outsider in this mainly White but changing school.

His name was Arnold Mireles, and he introduced himself to me the first day at that new school where I didn't know anyone. He was a little socially awkward and heavier like me, which was something we had in common. We quickly partnered to do art projects together because we both were budding artists. The teachers at the school asked students to draw artwork for the classrooms like holiday scenes for Easter or Christmas. Arnold and I would work together on the projects and conceive ideas together. I was a decent sketch artist, but nothing like Arnold Mireles.

123

He was so humble, but this kid could draw like a grownup. My stuff was decent, but Arnold had an eye for detail. He introduced me to "perspective," something he learned at an art school supply store on Commercial Avenue called Gitter & Siovic, a.k.a. Gitter's. We took art lessons there together when we got older. On most days, we were comparing artwork and being best buds. We were just two portly kids going through life together. I don't know if we ever really made the distinction that he was Mexican and I was Black, but it clearly never mattered!

Soon we would be visiting each other's homes. I needed my parents' permission to spend time at another kid's house because of their rule that it was necessary for them to meet the parents of all of my friends. One day, my parents met Arnold's parents, José and Guadalupe Mireles, at a school meeting and recognized a good family, so our friendship was ratified.

Arnold had a big Roman Catholic family with brothers and sisters who also attended Saints Peter and Paul. His sister Evelyn, also known as Belina, was in my sister Ramona's class three years behind me, and Sonia was in my sister Vanessa's class two years behind me. Jaime, also known as James, was a year older than me. He was in the same class as my friend Cathy when she later transferred to Saints Peter and Paul. The baby boys of the Mireles family, Albert and David, were a bit younger.

Once I started hanging out at the Mireles home, we would listen to music that I heard on WLS radio like Kiss and Boston. As we got older, I didn't keep up as much with my art skills because I became more motivated by science, while Arnold truly sharpened his art skills during those years.

Arnold was also a craftsman who did woodworking, a skill that he used in apartment buildings in South Chicago that his father, José, owned and managed. Arnold learned those woodworking skills from his father, who worked at U.S. Steel but also was an outstanding carpenter and artisan. Arnold's mom, Lupe, was a stay-at-home mom who spoke little to no English.

Through my Mexican friend, I learned about San Luis Potosí, Mexico, where his parents met and married before migrating to America. It was so similar to how my parents migrated from Nashville to Chicago. We had so much in common. Our friendship made some of the challenges of those days so much easier. We would unfortunately learn that some people around us didn't think people so different should be friends, but we ignored that nonsense. Unfortunately, racism would remain a constant in my educational experience during those years.

Saints Peter and Paul School was an overall better experience then Warren School, but far from perfect. This was really made apparent when it was time to recognize students at the school. I was passed over a number of times. White resentment and envy raised its head toward me in the fourth grade, which was my second year at Saints Peter and Paul.

While Whites were fleeing the area and moving further east to communities in Northwest Indiana like Dyer and St. John, or west to Oak Lawn and Orland Park, racial tensions were revealing themselves more and more frequently in South Chicago as Blacks and Hispanics were increasing in numbers in the community.

The economic reality for Whites was changing as Japanese steel was starting to supplant American steel and good-paying steel mill jobs were leaving U.S. communities like those on the Southeast Side of Chicago and in Northwest Indiana, or in towns like East Chicago and Gary. At the height of the steel industry, there were easily 30 or more steel factories within 10 miles with good paying jobs in those areas.

That all started changing in the mid-1970s when the area had a large Polish immigrant population and started experiencing racial tension. These folks seemed to have more problems with their new Brown and Black neighbors. Some of the Polish folks seemed to blame the decline of the community on people of color, when the reality was that jobs were simply leaving. It seems that there is a similar sentiment in 2021 on America's southern border where many White citizens work and live today.

Even with its challenges, Saints Peter and Paul had become my "fortress of solitude" in a sometimes cruel world. Mi Amigo Arnold Mireles made living in a changing world "bonito!" I also think I was seeing the heart and soul of a great artist and future community activist in Arnold Mireles as he was being molded in grammar school. He was a kind soul and would help anyone in need that he could.

Arnold loved his Mexican heritage and sketched all kinds of Aztec-inspired works for large paintings and even murals. He was so talented! There was an Aztec calendar mural in South Chicago that really inspired Arnold. He talked about one day painting one of those giant works of art. Arnold was also developing an eye for photography at this very young age.

We were so proud of each other after graduating from college. Two boys from the South Side were making our way in the world. With our humble starts in life, we both had come a long way and were the first in our respective families to graduate from college. Arnold graduated from Columbia College with a degree in Graphic Arts after attending St. Francis de Sales Catholic High School. I attended another Catholic high school, Quigley Preparatory Seminary South, then graduated from UIC with a psychology degree. By the time Arnold graduated from college, he was an exceptional artist. He showed me a portfolio of beautiful sketches and concepts he did while at Columbia College, which were out of this world. Arnold captured interesting images from all around Chicago, though he never learned to drive a car.

In one episode of *Good Times* titled "The Mural," J.J. painted a beautiful depiction of his neighborhood in a stunning mural on the wall of a community bank. That episode reminded me of the mural Arnold once spoke about painting in his South Chicago neighborhood. In the *Good Times* episode, a Black banker commissioned J.J. to paint a mural on the wall of his bank. But when the mural was completed, the banker did not like the work because he thought it was "too urban," and he threatened not to pay J.J. for it.

Not paying J.J. did not go over well with James Evans Sr. Patrons of the bank saw the unique piece of art and were amazed by it, and after some convincing from James Evans Sr., the banker ultimately paid J.J. James Evans had threatened to beat up the banker if he didn't pay his son, so the banker ultimately paid for J.J.'s work.

Good Times featured wonderful artwork by a black painter named Ernie Barnes. In my opinion, my friend Arnold was as good as Ernie Barnes. Arnold's artwork had the same kind of urban sensibility, but from the vantage point of a Mexican-American. Arnold also had some beautiful work in charcoal. I am certain that if given the chance, Arnold would have been able to paint his vision of his beloved South Chicago at South Chicago Bank located near our grammar school. On some days since first meeting my good friend, I feel like that banker who just did not appreciate the outstanding gift that this kid from South Chicago had and how visionary true art can be.

"ANYTIME YOU NEED A FRIEND."

Bishop Nevin W. Hayes, Arnold Mireles, and
I at our Confirmation as Roman Catholics
February 27, 1976
Saints Peter and Paul, Chicago 60617

128

CHAPTER 13
"The IQ Test"
Originally aired October 22, 1974

I started having issues at Saints Peter and Paul about the same time as an episode on Good Times called "The IQ Test" aired. In the episode, "Little" Michael comes home very upset, and his mom's maternal instincts kick in and she asks him what is wrong. Michael very reluctantly tells her that he flunked an IQ test given to him at school.

Florida knows that her child is very hardworking, so she believes that the test results must be wrong. As Michael's mother, she certainly is biased, but she is also an involved parent. Florida is a parent who pays attention to the academic pursuits of her children. You would never be able to tell this Black woman any untruths about her kids. Just like my mother!

By the fifth grade, I had become very comfortable in this very friendly, but academically challenging environment. At Saints Peter and Paul, precision and accuracy was stressed, along with studying very hard. Catholic education was also inherently religious in nature, and we were encouraged to pray while learning about Jesus and the Catholic faith.

Without the constant harassment from neighborhood bullies like in public school, I was able to thrive in my new environment. I soon began receiving recognition for being very competitive in terms of academics. I prided myself on getting 100s on tests and quizzes!

Mrs. Rogers, one of my favorite teachers, used to have a chart at the front of the class with all of our names on it. On that chart, stars would be placed by our names for perfect attendance and having the highest grades. I lived for those stars! Those grades also got me White Sox tickets, which was an added bonus.

Sr. Marilyn was my favorite nun and teacher. One day after reading in class, she asked me to do the readings at mass, and I was so honored. My family was converting to Catholicism, and I really wanted to fit in with the other Catholic kids. Sr. Marilyn taught me how to adjust a microphone and make eye contact when reading and speaking publicly at a lectern. She said "breathe" and "always practice something before you read it." I continue to do those things to this day.

Sr. Marilyn was such a sweetheart. Because my mother was at the school quite often, she seemed to really like our family. My mother once mentioned to her how she wished she was better at gardening because she struggled with flowers. My grandmother Roberta, who had the greenest of thumbs, used to plant flowers for my mom when she visited Chicago, but she only came to Chicago once a year or so. Sr. Marilyn liked my mom so much that she and another nun came over to our house on Jeffery and planted beautiful flowers at our home one year.

Everything was wonderful at that school until "it" started happening again. I was doing quite well in school and received first honors beginning in the fourth grade, but my parents noticed that some teachers were writing odd comments in the subjective portion of my report cards .At that school, once you reached the sixth grade and read at an advanced level, you could qualify for a special reading program where sixth, seventh and eighth-grade students studied together. When I reached the sixth grade, my Iowa test scores indicated that I was reading at a twelfth-grade level, so I qualified to become a part of the program. I believe that being an avid reader is why I had a great vocabulary and reading ability, which paved the way for me to be put in the group.

I met a transfer student named Cathy in that program. She was the sister of my future best buddies from high school. Cathy was in the seventh grade, a year ahead of me. We became friends and have a friendship to this day. She and my wife Denise would meet while they were residents at Cook County Hospital.

I loved science as much as reading, so I couldn't wait to compete in the annual science Fair the school hosted each year. I loved the thought of this contest. I remember to this day a science project I designed that was out of this world. My topic was about Louis Pasteur and the pasteurization process of the milk delivered to a local grocery store like Jewel Foods.

I meticulously sketched out the layout for the exhibit at the kitchen table. The exhibit showed step by step the process from milking cows and pasteurization all the way to milk trucks delivering the product to your local grocery store. I wanted my project to have moving parts, so I borrowed my dad's chicken rotisserie motor to rotate the stage like a carousel. It was like the theater in the round at the Mill Run Theatre in suburban Niles.

Mom brought home little procaine injection bottles from the hospital that I used to simulate dairy bottles. She suggested I use butterfly IV tubing to simulate being connected to the udders of cows for milking. I used a syringe to remove the procaine and injected the little clear bottles with powdered milk to simulate the milk.

The exhibit had battery-operated lights from Radio Shack, and it was as big as a card table. I felt like Peter Brady and his volcano. I did it by myself! Everyone who saw it was amazed! There were a lot of entries, but none like mine.

My parents were so proud until the judges put a second prize ribbon on my project. I went home dejected. My dad didn't say much on the ride home, and Mom had a funny look on her face. I remember Cathy once recalling something similar happening to her at St. Ailbe School, which is why she transferred. Catholic school was nice, but not perfect.

For the next couple of years, only white students were given the first-place honors at the annual awards assembly. At the same time, the school was becoming more diverse with students of many races who were doing well in their studies. New Black and Brown students were routinely getting passed over for the top honors.

I consistently received the highest grades in my class on my tests and quizzes, but would always have my grades discounted by some subjective item on my report card. One year I was given an "F" for a pinhole camera, though I was a master of science projects. And messing up a camera? My parents knew I loved cameras, especially after visiting my aunt Louise and my play uncle Rochester in Rochester, New York. My play uncle Rochester and Uncle Bert Wilson worked for Kodak. Uncle Bert was married to Carole, and they had three children, Robert, Kenneth and Veronica.

The Kodak brand was like Tide detergent in our house. We had all kind of Kodak cameras, including a Super 8 movie camera. I relished the idea of making a camera, so when a teacher failed me for not knowing how to make a pinhole camera, my parents knew that something was amiss. In fact, I had already made a pinhole camera in my Cub Scout troop.

Another teacher lowered a grade because I supposedly didn't turn in a poster. I was very meticulous with my designs for class projects, and I spent so much money at Gitter's and Par Drugs on poster boards and stencils that they should have named a brand after me. I would sometimes see Cathy's dad, who worked as a butcher at Par Drugs. Using stencils was a lot of work because before there were desktop computers which have hundreds of fonts, there were cardboard stencils with very few fonts like Roman and Gothic. It required a lot of work picking out text styles and making words straight with cardboard stencils.

I had been working hard ever since I arrived at that school. My mom was always at the school and kept track of the homework my sisters and I brought home. If we didn't do school work, that was a punishable offense. My parents knew their kids' abilities and work habits very well.

By the time I reached the seventh grade, my parents were very suspicious about what some teachers were saying about their eldest child. My parents felt some things were not adding up, so once again, they found themselves at a desk talking to a White principal about their young Black son. My dad had all my report cards and piles of tests and quizzes when they met with the principal, Fr. Robert McNamara, and they wanted answers!

Fr. Mac, a very young new priest, had just taken over as principal after Sr Petronet retired. He was previously the chaplain at St. Bernard Hospital, located a short distance from the postal station when Dad worked there. My dad knew people around St. Bernard who said that he was a nice guy. They also assured him that he wasn't likely racist as he had worked in "the hood" before coming to Saints Peter and Paul.

My parents had a discussion about the events over the last few years with their kids, but Fr. Mac made a statement that implied some people in the school might have a problem with their son being ranked number one even though the world was changing around them. My parents received a very strong message without another word being said.

He was really a nice guy and not a racist, but my parents felt that he was giving in to racism. My parents were paying a lot of money for three kids to attend that school! Fr. Mac left the priesthood after a few years. My dad mentioned years later that the good Father had a female "friend" or two on his route, which might explain his change in careers.

My parents then transferred my sisters and me to neighboring St. Joseph. The thing that made that move harder than any other was that I had to leave behind my best buddy in the whole world, Arnold Mireles!

"TEMPORARY LAYOFF!"

Me in my Cub Scout uniform (lower right)
Beverly Evangelical Lutheran Church, 91st and Jeffery
Calumet Heights, Chicago 60617 Circa 1971

CHAPTER 14
"Breaker, Breaker!"

Originally aired November 9, 1977

The 1970s were, if anything, about fads. We wore big Afros and bell bottom pants. The hottest dance moves would be copied from *Soul Train*, and we all hung out at record stores like Metro Music and Coop's on 87th Street to listen to the latest cuts before digging into the rows of 45s. My dad knew the Black owner of a record store on his mail route on 71st and Halsted, and the owner used to give him 45s that he would bring home.

I loved music as much as science and reading, and I used to spend a lot of the money I made cutting grass and doing minor home repairs on records. I loved records and couldn't wait to pick the latest hot record at Metro Music. While my dad was able to get a lot of 45s for free from the record store on his route, we had to buy any albums. In record stores, the hottest albums were kept behind the counter. I loved anything that was created by Earth, Wind & Fire. This band was created by Mr. Maurice White of Chicago during this great era of music. In my opinion, Earth, Wind & Fire is the greatest group ever! Fight me!

My wife took me to an Earth, Wind & Fire concert that included three of the original members. Verdine White, Philip Bailey and Ralph Johnson were leading the group at that Chicago concert. It was a good show, but a little sad because you could tell the group missed their former leader and founder Maurice White, who had just passed away a couple of months before that concert. His brother Verdine White fell off the stage during the show, but being the consummate professional, jumped up and kept it moving without missing a beat.

The highlight of that evening was when Denise arranged for me to meet those three remaining founding members after the show. We were able to take a photo with them, and Philip Bailey graciously signed a copy of his book for me. The group Chicago was the lead act at that concert and sounded even better than on my cousin Cedric's reel-to-reel!

When I was about 13 years old, my main hobby was CBing. Citizens band radios or CBs were the Twitter and Facebook of the 1970s. One of the best-known manufacturers of CBs at that time was Chicago-based Cobra Radio. Many chimneys around the city had CB antennas mounted on them. Real big-timers had 30- and 40-foot aluminum towers with rotating directional antennas called "beams" on them. A popular brand was the Avanti Moonraker 4, which was used to focus radio signals to faraway distances. I had an Avanti Moonraker 4 atop a 30-foot tower in front of our home. That tower was installed by myself and some CB buddies on top of a large block of concrete covering a 55-gallon drum buried in the ground.

My hobby included meeting with local CB clubs and reading CB magazines. Each club would claim a specific CB channel amongst 40 AM and 80 Single Sideband (SSB) to operate from. Daily chatter included the news or the latest "haps" in the hood. Many club members had both mobile units in their cars and base units at home. "Legal" CBs straight out of the box had the power of 4 watts on AM and 12 watts on SSB.

The range was about 10 miles on AM channels and 75 miles on SSB, if there weren't too many people. We CBers had to learn how to be mini technicians and do things like fix the standing wave ratio (SWR) of our antennas or adjust capacitors in the unit to modulate the right amount of wattage to drive the linear optimally. Linears were illegal amplifiers that produced at least 50 watts, which was 12 times the power of a stock radio. Most of us purchased illegal amplifiers that produced upwards of 2000 watts. I had one made by Maco that produced 500 watts. When you hit the air with that kind of power, you basically owned a radio station that you personally programed, which fit my personality perfectly.

If you walked down any sidewalk in the mid-1970s, you would see a multitude of chimney and roof-mounted CBs from Radio Shack and various mail-order electronics magazines. Every CBer was a part of small communities with a myriad of alter egos known as handles. Your CB handle was your persona or alias. Black CBers in my area had handles like Rerun and Showboat, and broadcast on Channel 22, while White CBers from the Far East Side used Channel 14. Segregation was alive and well even on CBs.

CBers had a unique language, especially amongst the foul-mouthed truck drivers who used Channel 19. Smokey The Bear was a police officer. 10-1 meant your signal was weak. 10-99 was an emergency. If you had an emergency, you were supposed to use Channel 9. A beaver was both a girl and a sex organ.

Conversations on the CB ranged from the mundane to the insane. One White female CBer from the Southeast Side with the handle Angel Face frequented on Channel 14. She often would talk about living in "slag valley," in reference to the steel mills in that area (slag was a byproduct of molten steel). At one time, there were five active steel mills on the Southeast Side of Chicago. The sky on the Southeast Side had a familiar orange hue at night from the steam of molten steel rising into the sky and turning the sky orange. At night, it had the effect of appearing like a sunrise over an operating mill. The stench in the air was unforgettable. Our neighborhood often smelled liked "the funk of 40,000 years" because of those mills!

For years, it has been speculated that the increased asthma and cancer rates seen in people from the surrounding communities might be related to pollutants from these mills. Altgeld Garden is a public housing complex located on the southernmost border of Chicago, at 130th Street. Residents have long blamed both the steel mills and a nearby Ford Automotive plant for polluting their environment and making their residents sick. Since we are talking about Black and Brown people, we have reason to be suspicious. The Tuskegee Experiment is always on our minds! In recent years, the air quality of the area has improved as those factories have all been closed down.

South Chicago and Northwest Indiana for many years provided an economic engine for the region and a great standard of living for employees at the various factories that manufactured steel for the auto industry. That all ended as these mills were undercut by cheap Japanese steel flooding the U.S. market.

When I attended dental school 25 years later, one of my classmates Jose Pedroza's father had worked for one of these mills for many years. An unfortunate accident occurred where one of the vats of molten steel traveling overhead on a track tipped over. Its contents poured to the ground where Jose's dad was standing and killed him instantly! That industry has a history of a lot of accidents that have killed employees.

Jose Pedroza and Genaro "Gino Rockin'" Romo were my two best friends during dental school. They were both Mexican-American and, like me, wanted to represent their communities of color in the best light in the field of dentistry. They helped me keep my sanity while we were going through the fire that was dental school.

Gino had local fame as a DJ on WYCC, a local radio station in the Little Village community of Chicago. He successfully managed dental school while also DJing parties on the weekend. From time to time when we were on break from dental school, I used to mess around on his turntables in his parents' Little Village home. It was like what I used to do with my buddies Kenton and Byron Samuels back in Hyde Park when we worked at the University of Chicago Hospital. Today, Gino is a successful dentist, and he also maintains a popular Facebook page where he still DJs.

In the *Good Times* episode "Breaker, Breaker!" Michael assumes the alter ego of his brother J.J. to impress a female CBer named Fun Girl. During the episode, Michael finds out that the young lady he was making all of these big dating plans with, including skating and dancing actually used a wheelchair. Michael was himself a flawed hypocrite who was lying about his own position in life, and he dared not want to date an imperfect person in spite of his own imperfections and lies. The episode forced Michael to come to grips with the fact that he also was a flawed person.

J.J. implores Michael to do the right thing and be honest to the young lady. By the end of the episode, Michael faces his lies and those of Fun Girl. The episode ends with him telling this young lady the truth about himself. Mike matured by willing to be honest and vulnerable. He ultimately became the young man he was always capable of being. His proud older brother J.J. congratulates him for his "rite of passage" into adulthood in a very touching closing scene.

I could relate to Michael as I was a preteen approaching high school age and beginning the process of defining my identity during those turbulent adolescent years. CBing allowed me to create an alternative reality. CB was like a fantasyland where we could "jack our jaws" and plan exciting, even if imaginary, adventures. How much lying occurs on Facebook every day now?

Because of CBing, I actually worked on my public speaking skills that I use in my life today. I also learned to interact with different types of people and connect with people all around the country and outside the country, even as far as Jamaica and the Bahamas, with that setup in my bedroom. I also met a lot of cool people at CB rallies.

On my radio, I was like Herb Kent, my favorite DJ, in my little part of the world. I had to work out broadcast times with my neighbors because my CB with its illegal linear used to tear up TV stations on my block. I made a pact with our neighbors to broadcast during non-soap opera hours to avoid nasty looks from them. Channel 2 was the most susceptible to my broadcasts, and my mom watched *As the World Turns* like the rest of the neighbors.

When "Breaker, Breaker!" came on my TV, it reminded me that I also was coming of age and experiencing my own rite of passage. We all have to learn to be honest and deal with life's challenges in our own ways.

"FUN GIRL, YOU ARE COMING IN REAL 10-8!"

Just lookin' out of the window

CHAPTER 15
"Crosstown Buses Run All Day, Doodah, Doodah"

Originally aired October 1, 1974

Good Times was a very interesting sociological experiment that played out on TV. Even though the show was based on a Black family, it had mainly White writers. One of the writers was Joe Bonaduce, the father of Danny Bonaduce, a.k.a. Danny Partridge of the Partridge Family. It is likely that the higher-ups at CBS took comfort in knowing that White writers would probably not get too controversial in dealing with Black topics. At the same time, Mr. Paul Mooney also wrote episodes for the show, as well as writing for comedian Richard Pryor, and was known to take issues of race head on.

Though writers were not always as culturally diverse in the 1970s, the writers did try to deal with racism during the course of the show. When the writers of "Crosstown Buses Run All Day" conceived that episode, it seems like the goal was to highlight disparities in access to educational resources using the character Michael while not being too controversial, as busing was a third rail at that time.

In the episode, the Evans family finds themselves torn when Michael has outgrown the resources in his local school. He is given an opportunity to attend a better school across town in a White community which required busing. The episode also touched on racism and the concept that White communities often have access to better schools.

Viewers of the episode would indirectly ponder the question of "Why do Black communities have such failing schools? Is it because Blacks are less intelligent?" Also, racism is systemic and enabled. Most

Whites are certainly not racists, but many are enablers of racism. What does an enabler of racism look like? It is the White neighbor who assumes that your highly intelligent Black children were accepted into a top university just because they are Black.

It is also the passive enabler who witnesses or is aware of a racist act, but says nothing because "it" doesn't impact them. Our police forces have repeatedly shown that racist policing results in disproportionate harm to Blacks when we encounter law enforcement. When I was a young student at Joseph Warren many years ago, the White students who hurt me and angered me more than the bullies were the majority of the Whites in the school who just watched or turned their collective heads as I was being attacked.

Those White students who stood by and said nothing as I was being tormented let the small population of jerks in your midst run amok! George Floyd would tragically learn this as the life was kneeled out of his body, while other cops watched it happen, including an Asian officer. Some in that same Asian population are now seeking solidarity with Blacks as they are now being victimized by other racists.

When I grew up in Chicago, there were arbitrary boundaries placed between the races. Black people can't live here or marry that person over there. Aside from being dangerous, systemic racism often prevents people of color from accessing good schools or even a decent store with fruits and vegetables in their community.

One border I crossed in the fifth or sixth grade occurred in pursuit of my tropical fish hobby. I normally purchased fish for my aquarium from Goldblatt's or Woolworth's, which were both near my school. I wanted some Black Angelfish that neither store sold, so I decided to go to this fancy store advertised in the local phone book called the East Side Water Garden.

This store was located on the far east side past 95th and the Calumet River, an unofficial border that Blacks didn't cross at the time. My parents often warned me to never go east of that border. But I didn't listen! As they say, a hard head makes a soft behind! I decided that I was going to go to the East Side even after being told how Big Walter had been harassed a few times coming from his job at Commonwealth Edison (ComEd) in Calumet Park, just east of that bridge, in his nice Cadillac.

In spite of the danger, one Saturday morning I started the day off with a lie to my parents. I told them that I was going to my friend Arnold's house as I did most Saturdays, but the reality was I had another plan. I had a pocket full of money and was going to buy some giant Black Angelfish from the pet store pictured in that phone book ad, so I placed the folded-up ad in my pocket that morning and hit the road. I walked a route east until I reached the front of Calumet Fisheries, a popular place to purchase fried fish products at 95th and the Calumet River. This is the place that I was told to *never* pass!

A 12-year-old, overweight Black kid started walking across a forbidden bridge for those special fish. People in passing cars gave me some weird looks, but I was oblivious and continued on my way to that pet store. My hell began about halfway over the bridge when three White boys about 15 or 16 years of age asked me, "Where are you going, nigger?" This gave me immediate flashbacks of getting beat up at Warren. I was also a little shocked because I hadn't been called a nigger in quite a while.

I replied, "I am going to the pet store to get some fish!" That statement alone probably should have gotten my ass kicked for saying "pet store." I then pulled that folded ad out of my pocket and showed one of the guys, and then the other two started gut punching me. They emptied out the money in my pockets. Just like the old days. I was scared and wanted to run, but they had me!

After they got most of the money out of my pocket, some of the coins fell into the Calumet River. I started screaming for help, and at that point, they tried to throw me over the railing into the river, but fortunately, because I was a little portly, they couldn't lift me. The one time that I was glad to be a fat boy! I was holding on to the railing for dear life! I was just fat enough that they couldn't get me over that railing.

I thought I was going to die until a blue City of Chicago garbage truck with two Black guys in it pulled up to get food at Calumet Fisheries. None of the White people who saw me getting attacked on that bridge came to help, but thankfully, the Black dudes jumped out of the truck, grabbed a shovel and told those White dudes to leave me alone, and those White boys got out of there! One of the Black workers asked me if I was "a damn fool" for being over there. He asked me where I lived and took me back to 95th South Chicago in the "Black safe zone."

I then went to Arnold's house to hang out. I didn't tell him or my family what happened that day until years later. I actually didn't walk on that bridge until many years later either. That experience made me realize that real racism is a life-and-death matter.

"KEEPING YOUR HEAD ABOVE WATER!"

CHAPTER 16
"The Family Gun"
Originally aired September 16, 1975

Violence in urban areas is routinely seen in stories featured on local news broadcasts. Unfortunately, when people think about our major metropolitan areas like New York, Detroit, St. Louis or my hometown of Chicago, images of violence spontaneously flow into their minds.

When people say the name "Chicago," they often reference the violent era of Prohibition when a ruthless Al Capone ruled the streets. His murderous act of killing his mob enemies in front of the Biograph Theater was memorialized in the movie called The *St. Valentine's Day Massacre*. Unfortunately, violent street crime is an everyday thing in the streets of Chicago in 2021.

For many years, Chicago has been an epicenter of gun violence. Several episodes of *Good Times* dealt with guns. In the episode "The Family Gun," James has purchased a gun to protect his family. He becomes concerned when his gun turns up missing and a nearby resident is shot with a gun fitting the description of his missing gun. James is very distraught about the prospect of possibly misplacing a gun that might have injured a neighbor. In real life, many gang shootings result in the killing of an innocent college student home for spring break or a pregnant mother who happens to end up in the line of fire. By the end of the episode, viewers are relieved to find out that Michael had moved the gun for safekeeping and the gun was not involved in any crime.

People often cite the Second Amendment of the U.S. Constitution as guaranteeing the rights of all to bear arms for protection, which is true unless you are the Black Panthers and Ronald Reagan is the governor of the State of California. The proliferation of guns has become a problem in our country, resulting in many senseless shootings. Mass shootings are now a regular occurrence in schools across our nation, often with military-grade weapons. People from all political stripes debate the necessity of possessing guns to protect our families against the absolute right to own weapons of war like the AR-15. This military weapon was designed to shoot multiple rounds and easily kill many people on the battlefield. It was never intended for use by the avid deer hunter or to be kept in the home to stop a domestic invader.

Most reasonable people are okay with people legally owning handguns and rifles for self-defense and hunting purposes. The argument over possession of these guns often involves gun enthusiasts who want to be able to own any type of gun while putting everyone in danger. Most gun owners actually support reasonable gun legislation, but organizations like the National Rifle Association (NRA) control the public narrative.

The first time I saw a gun was when my play uncle Rochester was visiting us with my Aunt Louise. When he came to visit, he would ask my father to keep his revolver in a gun box and secure it in the closet of my parents' room. Because the gun was being stored in their bedroom during these visits, my parents told my sisters and me that their room was off limits. I got a glimpse of the gun once while Dad was safely putting it out of the reach of us kids.

The first time I had a gun pulled on me was when I worked as a stock boy for S.S. Kresge at 63rd and Halsted. The store was part of the Kmart chain. This job involved my first foray in driving as a young adult because I used to drive to work in my first car. The hand-me-down car was the family's old red Pinto station wagon that we travelled to Nashville in many times. My dad worked a few blocks away as a mail carrier at the Englewood Post Office located at 611 West 63rd Street.

At Kresge, I made a couple of new friends on this job who were much different from the people I grew up with. My co-workers were really cool guys, including one dude named King Mayes who went to Harlan High School. He was older than me, but he let me hang out with him and the guys after work. When I worked at Kresge, I really liked making my own money. It was also a chance to work in a community very similar to mine but different as well. Most of the folks who worked there were from Englewood and worked at this job to support their families.

My stock boy co-workers were mainly about my age and in high school, while some were a little older at 18 or 19. It was an adventure for me hanging out after work with those guys. We checked out movies at the Englewood Theater down the block on payday. I had a lot of fun roaming the store and flirting with girls with my work crew.

Our stock boy duties included running the "blue light specials": "Attention Kresge shoppers, we are having a special on S-Curl in aisle 3!" After the announcement, there would be a mad dash by the hair care items in aisle 3. We were responsible for stocking the aisles with needed items. We also had to bring boxes of Brach's candy down from the upstairs stock room and place loose pieces of candy in the various bins. This candy was sold individually or by the pound.

Because the store had a little lunch counter and the loose candy, it also had a little rat problem. As stock boys, we had to address the problem during "rat detail" to look for rats before and after the store closed. The rat detail had three parts. Part one was to make bait for the rats. We sliced cooked hot dogs from the lunch counter in half and poured Drano into them in the alley behind the store. We nicknamed them "Drano Dogs." Part two was placing them around the store at closing time when the store had no customers. Part three occurred in the mornings before the store opened, when we had to go around the store and shovel up the dead little "furry fellows."

Paydays were the best because we were paid in cash in little manila envelopes. After picking up our cash, we used to go in the little shops on Halsted and buy some fashionable polyester shirts for possible dating situations we might encounter. One of my first girlfriends was a cashier who worked at Kresge and lived nearby on Morgan. I went to her junior prom at Visitation Catholic High School.

On one of these paydays while we were in line outside the cashier getting our loot, this dude with a ski mask ran up to the front of the line and pulled out a gun and screamed, "Give me your money!" I was like "I'll be damned" in my head, but when he pointed the barrel of that gun at me, I threw that manila envelope of cash in that bag he had like everyone else in line!

At this point, the crime turned into an episode of *Scooby-Doo* because folks in the line recognized the dude in the ski mask as a co-worker. Then one of the White store managers jumped him from behind and got the gun from him, which turned out not to be loaded. Our manager pulled the mask off his head, and when his big Afro popped out, there was one of my fellow stock boys. He was no Kareem Akbar, an educated kid from the bank, but a dumb dude from the hood who just committed a felony!

I can't remember his name, but we both were the same age. He had a father who recently left him and his mom, and he was just trying to get some extra money. He actually looked a little like that guy Mad Dog who shot J.J. in one episode. When the police came, they took him to the Audy Home, a Chicago detention center for underaged kids, because he was too young to go to Cook County Jail. I never saw that guy again, but I knew the mistake he made would change his life. I pray that it got better for him. As for me, I didn't touch a gun until I was an adult in the U.S. Army Reserves, when I was required to train with a 9mm revolver to potentially defend myself from a foreign invader even though I was serving as a dentist.

"OOH, J.J., YOU'RE IN TROUBLE!"

CHAPTER 17
"The Gang: Part 1"

Originally aired November 12, 1974

Guns and violence had unfortunately become a mainstay in American cities in the post-Civil Rights 1970s. When *Good Times* aired the episodes "The Gang (Parts 1 and 2)," they presented an unfortunate reality that is so commonplace today, because most families know a victim of gun violence.

At the end of the episode, the wounded J.J. is being held by his father as his mother is screaming for help after he has just been shot. This scene would be repeated over and over again in real streets of real cities. What does constant violence do to the psyche of a Black community plagued by it daily?

John Singleton directed the cult classic *Boyz* n the Hood, which depicts that urban reality with the insight that only one who has witnessed such horror firsthand can achieve. Though the chief victim Ricky resided in South Central Los Angeles, the same scene occurs on a daily basis in every major city in the U.S. today.

As the 1970s proceeded into the 1980s, shootings increased in Black communities at an alarming rate. The Englewood community was in the national news for the extraordinary number of shootings in the late '80s. There were hundreds of people getting shot mainly on the West and South sides of Chicago every summer, and Englewood became the epicenter. This was the very community in which my father was a letter carrier in for many years. Things had changed dramatically in that area over the years.

More than 1000 people died one summer during the '80s in Chicago. We as a family worried each day that my father might become a victim on his Englewood route, which eventually prompted him to retire early at 55 years of age from his beloved postal job. Around the same time my dad decided to retire, a co-worker at my next job at the University of Chicago Bernard Mitchell Hospital named Ray Gatson was shot for his car at a car wash near the hospital.

By the 1980s, many of the Black businesses in Englewood were being bought out by new Middle Eastern owners. My father worked part-time at a bar/liquor store on his route until the Black owner sold to some of these new immigrants. My father noticed that some of these new owners didn't treat the Black clientele with the same level of respect. Often these new owners would come into the community and profit from it while mistreating the citizens who generated their middle-class lifestyles and wealth. Racism is indeed in play in these situations where the new Brown business owners disrespect the Black community that they are profiting off of. Because the Black customers often lack transportation, they continued to return to these same businesses to shop. All news was not bad, however, because a Black family named Callahan became the new owners of the mortuary on Halsted. That family has done many good things for the Black residents of Englewood over the years, including the creation of a foundation to assist needy students.

The Englewood Concourse on 63rd and Halsted, which included my old employer Kresge, was once a hub of activity with stores like Hillman Grocery and Nelson Brothers Furniture Store, but it was shuttered in the mid-1980s. My parents' own community was not immune to the economic changes occurring on the South Side. It began with low-level crimes like car break-ins, but it soon graduated to drug-related crimes. "Hypes" and "crackheads" all trying to find small things to sell for drugs became very common. Some bum broke into my car and stole my best Farley Keith house tapes. Savages! Car break-ins escalated to home break-ins and robberies on the street. The innocence of the community of my youth was being lost. That hurt my soul!

The thing that changed my view of that wonderful community forever, was the rape of a family friend by someone dubbed the "Pill Hill rapist." I remember when my friend's brother sat in my living room and told me that his sister had been raped by that asshole! He was so angry, and so was I! I felt his pain every bit as much as if she was my sister. He wanted to kill that guy, so we got in his car to search for that criminal. I got in that car with my friend, even though I was hoping NOT to find him. I was prepared to prevent my friend from taking matters into his own hands! Thankfully, law enforcement found and prosecuted that criminal. The die had been cast for me relative to that community, and I wanted out! My safe haven was no more! I never wanted to live in my beloved community after that.

While working at the University of Chicago, I started hanging out in Hyde Park and became good friends with two co-workers, Byron and Kenton, who lived in that community. They were graduates of Kenwood High and knew Hyde Park very well. We hung out at all the cool neighborhood spots. Their community was so much like my neighborhood when we first moved in, but the Whites stayed in Hyde Park.

Our main hangout was their parents' Hyde Park condo. There, we tinkered on our cars and mixed house music on Kenny's turntables. Kenny was a popular DJ at Kenwood High School and around Hyde Park. Kenny loved his Volkswagen Beetles that he drove while sporting his Dwayne Wayne flip glasses. Hyde Park was a university community protected by both the University of Chicago campus police and the Chicago Police.

It was not hard to miss the disparity in violence in that community compared to my own, which was only about 15 minutes south. As soon as any major crime occurred, multiple police resources were Johnny on the Spot in Hyde Park. Since a significant portion of the community remained White, I think that accounts for the differences between that community and other South Side communities, including mine.

When my dad decided to take his retirement at the age of 55, because of the increase in crime, he and my mom moved to the South

Suburbs. After 30 years of city life, my folks moved into their second home in Lynwood located just west of the Indiana border. They were, once again, some of the first Black residents of that bedroom community when they arrived in 1987.

It was time for a new start in their second home out of public housing. It was time for new adventures and hopefully an escape from the increasing violence of Chicago. Another rainbow, another pot of gold!

"MAKING A WAVE WHEN YOU CAN!"

My parents' 2nd home in Lynwood, Illinois 60411

CHAPTER 18
"A Place to Die"
Originally aired December 30, 1975

Michael Evans was the character on *Good Times* who most reminded me of myself. He was always quoting some Black leader or some book that he was reading at the time. He was so aptly nicknamed the "militant midget" for always being outspoken and speaking truth to power.

Michael Evans was always standing up to adults at great personal risk, even if it meant talking back to his father, who definitely didn't like that! He ran the risk of getting "The Big Mac" if he truly pissed off James Evans Sr. Occasionally, he would set his father's short fuse off, but always from a place of love. I had the same tendency with my own father.

One day, Michael brought home an older guest for dinner. The guest was an old guy from the neighborhood; they had become friends. The man was obviously lonely and had no family, but Michael, with his childlike innocence, wanted to bring him by for a meal. Though not the same, I had a penchant for bringing strays home. My strays were animals, not human beings, though!

One of our family's most famous animal adventures was when I smuggled a kitten in a shoebox back to Chicago after one of our summer stays in Nashville. This was the summer that I stayed with Aunt Esther Owens Buchanan and her kids. Near her house were a bunch of stray cats running around that I would play with. I had become really fond of a little male calico kitten and decided that I was going to take it back to Chicago when it was time to go back home, though I knew my dad would never go for that. Dad never was a fan of dogs or cats, so getting the kitty back to Chicago would require a big smuggling caper.

The day my parents came to pick up my sisters and me to take us back home, I went down the street from my aunt's house, caught the little cat and popped him into a shoebox. I hid the cat out of sight. I put the shoebox in the back of the car on the floor between the front seat and back seat, under a pillow on the floor by our feet next to the transmission hump. I showed my sisters the stowaway. They giggled with excitement as we all chugged northbound on I-65.

That poor cat made it to just outside of Bowling Green, Kentucky, before he started whining in agony from the heat. That car had no air conditioning, so that cat got HOT! Also, the transmission hump gets really hot as well. That cat was half dead from the heat, and when we pulled over, my dad saw this cat and was pissed! He wanted to "put that damn cat on the side of the road!" My sisters and I were begging him to not do that. My mom eventually talked him into letting us bring the cat home instead of dumping it on the side of the road. We then took what would be our first pet cat home. Laddie became his name because I used to love watching Lassie and also liked when Scotty on Star Trek used that name.

On *Good Times*, Michael's newfound stray confided that he simply wanted a place to die, which was much more complicated than bringing a needy pet home. The request was more than a shock to Florida, who was being asked to do this act of mercy to a perfect stranger. Florida, like my mother, went along with the request.

The episode ends with the elderly gentleman falling to sleep and passing away peacefully around his adopted family at a party. There was something about death and how Florida held Michael in that episode that has always touched me and reminded me of how the love of a mother gets you through trying times as a kid and as an adult.

When we lived at 2611 S. Prairie, Mrs. Jane Milton was our family babysitter who cared for my sisters and me when our parents were at work. When my mom got off her job at Mercy across the street, my sisters and I would go out on the porch in front of Mrs. Milton's apartment and watch our mother coming out of the front door of the hospital. Mom would make her way home across the street wearing her customary scrubs, lab coat and bouffant cap.

Mrs. Milton was a widow who lived in a one-room apartment a couple doors down the hall from us on the seventh floor. She was older and walked using a cane. She had a roach problem, and her house smelled like those mothballs! She was basically a very sweet lady, but very stern. Over the years, my parents would become very close to her as she had no family.

They became so close that she asked my parents to take over her financial affairs. My dad would drive her out to her husband's gravesite at Mt. Glenwood in Glenwood, Illinois, every Veteran's Day. My dad also drove Mrs. Milton back to Mississippi on a number of occasions when members of her family passed away. She was so sad when we moved out of the projects, but Mom always visited her and took her grocery shopping. It was always nice to see her during the holidays when she came to our home. Mom often brought her out to our house for "family" dinners.

The concept of the village was strong in my parents. There have been so many family members who stayed with my parents at one time or another because of the way this couple from Nashville was built. After my parents moved to Lynwood, they moved Mrs. Milton in with them. Unfortunately, she developed dementia, and when she became very ill, my parents had to put her in a nursing home, where she died.

When she died, it was like we lost a part of our family and our past. That lady helped my family for many years. This woman had been an important part of our village for years, and I know my mother wanted this woman to know that she was loved, which is why she brought her home before she died.

In Africa, if a nomadic tribe had to move, it would only move as fast as its most elderly person. You should treasure the past that is the gift for the future.

"WATCHING THE ASPHALT GROW!"

155

Just lookin' out of the window

CHAPTER 19
"J.J. and the Plumber's Helper"

Originally aired December 2, 1978

In the episode "J.J. and the Plumber's Helper," J.J. loses the career that he had been working his whole life towards when he is fired as a graphic artist. The episode ends when J.J. meets an old flame named Vanessa, who was played by the glamorous "Dream Girl" Sheryl Lee Ralph. They go out on a date to a very expensive French restaurant, and she slips out on him when she finds out that J.J. is unemployed and can't afford dinner.

In that scene, you see a dejected J.J. slumped over at the dinner table, and the scene ends with his mom and Willona paying the bill and taking him home. You get a sense of the loss that J.J. was experiencing. He had lost a career that he had been dreaming about ever since that painting he did for "The Wiggler." Vanessa was so different from the other women he dated like "Delightful Delilah."

By this point in the *Good Times* television series, we have followed the many ups and downs that J.J. has experienced in his life. After finally establishing his career as an artist and even experiencing success in his romantic life, he felt like a failure. He had long gotten over being left in that hotel on his prom night by a heroin addict played by Debbie Allen. Remember that the first phone call he made that night was to his parents asking for their help.

Being an adult could truly be tough, as we saw through the years of the adventures of J.J. and his family. For me, I found my entrance into adulthood was relatively smooth. After graduation from high school,

I matriculated successfully on my own through college, the first in my family to do so. I went through that "adulting" process of trying to decide "what do I want to be when I grow up?" fairly well.

Four years after graduating from college in 1990, I would marry a childhood sweetheart from the old neighborhood and finally nail down the career pursuit that fit my calling in life, or so I thought. I became a suit-wearing manager for the "Good Hands" people at Allstate Insurance Company in their commercial division located in South Barrington, Illinois. After four years in a corporate setting, though, I realized that being a manager in corporate America really wasn't my thing.

I had never really given up on the idea from my college days of becoming some type of doctor. My dental appointments with my dentist and fraternity brother Allen Knox really solidified my interest in the career of dentistry. My old basketball buddy Larry had already begun his career as a dentist and was actually covering for Dr. Knox one day when I went for my appointment. Dr. Knox was in the Army Reserves and had been deployed to Kuwait as a part of Desert Storm. He had talked to me about pursuing the military as well.

While I was working my corporate job, my buddy Arnold and I wouldn't get to see each other much. Also, after I got married, I moved to suburban Arlington Heights, which was pretty far from the old neighborhood. I was also working on a Master of Business Administration (MBA) degree at the Water Tower Campus of Loyola University in Chicago, which also consumed a lot of my time.

Arnold and I still made an effort at Christmas to see each other, which is when I would see his parents. I was always hoping to be treated to a tasty batch of his mother Lupe's homemade tamales that she made for me every Christmas. Though she never really mastered English, she would always talk to me and treat me like family.

During this time, my wife and I would both quit our jobs and both return to school at UIC for new career pursuits. My wife was beginning a PhD in history, and I was in the midst of the DDS program. During the academic and mental struggles of this time, it became really hard for my wife and me.

Dental school was the hardest thing I had attempted up to that point in my life. When I started the program in the fall of 1993 at age 30, things became challenging. It was a hard time for both my wife and me, and a looming reality soon presented itself. My wife first came to the realization that it was not right for us to remain married. After that, things went from bad to worse! In November of 1994, while we were on winter break during the second year of our respective programs, I will never forget when my childhood sweetheart told me, "I don't want to be married anymore!"

In the end, divorce was just something that had to happen. We were presented with information that it would not be right for us to remain married. We both did our best under the circumstances, but the relationship needed to end, and that was very painful!

When my wife gave me the news that our marriage was over, I actually went to the movies and saw *Star Trek Generations*. In a plot twist that only real life could write, my beloved Captain Kirk was killed off in that movie. Talk about shitty timing! He was dead, and my marriage was dead! You can't escape death or a divorce when a marriage ends. There is no Kobayashi Maru in real life!

My wife and I started the separation process and ultimately divorced. During that time, I started failing dental school, and a few months later, both of us were standing before Judge Tim Evans, and the marriage was over! I felt like I had made every possible mistake that a so-called "smart person" could make. I ended up moving into the basement of my parents' house at the age of 32, which was pretty humiliating! I felt like a failure! I felt J.J.'s heartbreak and despair, and the feeling of having a worthless life and having to turn to my parents to bail me out! That sucked, but I did learn that sometimes pain helps you to grow and seek other opportunities.

Just like how J.J.'s mom picked him up, my family rallied around me. Out of that misery, I was forced to pick up the pieces of my life, focus on school and eventually became a leader in my dental class. I would actually obtain a couple of scholarships and some awards. I was asked to represent my dental school in establishing a partnership with Smith Barney and convinced them to provide dental scholarships to worthy students.

I still had my gift of charming folks and getting people to do things for me (just like Grandad Carl). As a result, I was the first student to receive this scholarship, and I talked them into funding a scholarship for the foreseeable future. I was also selected to be the National Minority Consultant for the American Student Dental Association (ASDA) and represented my school at their national convention in Louisville, Kentucky, in 1997.

By the end of dental school two years later, I would even find love again. Just like J.J. found his T.C. at the end of that episode who didn't care that he was broke and broken, I would meet a woman who took me in at my lowest. I met Dr. Denise Jackson, a fellow resident with my friend Cathy at Cook County Hospital. Cathy convinced me to go on a blind date with her new friend, Denise. We went on a group date with Cathy and most of her siblings to the Dixie Kitchen in Hyde Park, which was near the Hyde Park condo I owned. I wanted to live in that community for years, so I bought a place in the community while in dental school to start a new beginning.

Denise and I were studying in our respective programs two blocks from each other, but would never have met had it not been for the prodding of a mutual friend from my old neighborhood. God makes sure we all have "Good Times."

"Ain't we lucky we got 'em!"

Picture of Denise and I
Charcoal pencil rendering By Alpha Brother Isaac Castelaz

Just lookin' out of the window

CHAPTER 20
"The Gang: Part 2"

Originally aired November 19, 1974

In "The Gang: Part 2," "Mad Dog" has shot J.J. for not being willing to join a gang. In that episode, we see how the lives of the victims of gun violence are forever changed. Many young Black men in real life are forced to join gangs or be killed in our cities. Admittedly, when this happened on *Good Times*, it wasn't real. Also, in that episode J.J. is shot, but he lives to see another day. How many are shot in real life but don't survive? In real life when a real gunshot hits real flesh, real damage is done. That damage doesn't go away at the end of a 30-minute episode.

I was at one the highest points in my life when I obtained a Doctorate of Dental Surgery (DDS) in 1997. I had come a long way from that seventh-floor apartment in public housing. Tough life experiences forced me to learn that we all have to go through some rough times to get to where we ultimately are supposed to be.

My friend Arnold was also finding his way in life as a very gifted artist and photographer who had developed a passion for community activism. He had a variety of his works commissioned as murals throughout South Chicago. His father also owned a number of rental properties in South Chicago that Arnold helped him to manage.

Arnold lived in one of his family's properties, a Victorian building on Exchange Avenue three blocks from our old grammar school. It was a building with elegant stained-glass windows and beautiful woodwork and pocket doors. Arnold could tell you the history of his building and those in the surrounding neighborhood because he loved Chicago, especially South Chicago.

Arnold had grown up to be that guy who picked up garbage off of the sidewalk for neighbors and would help anyone in need. He was very proud of his Mexican heritage. He truly loved people and was a proud American and Chicago citizen.

Arnold didn't like what was happening to his neighborhood. As nuclear families were starting to disappear, gang bangers began selling their drugs in his community and unfamiliar faces began hanging out on the stoops of surrounding properties. Arnold wasn't fazed by the "New Jack" drug revolution occurring in South Chicago, and he began to work at an area community center that was committed to making South Chicago a great community again.

There were still signs of life on Commercial Avenue, where many Mexican-Americans had thriving businesses. September 16th was a big holiday as the neighborhood was emblazoned with flags and music for Mexican Independence Day, and the same for Cinco de Mayo. But there was a dark underbelly in the streets, where crime was on the rise. Some landlords who purchased neighboring properties were not so caring about their tenants and properties. Some properties basically became "crack houses," but Arnold would keep up the good fight around his community.

If you met Arnold, you saw a simple innocence and his belief in the good of others. He would give you the shirt off of his back. Whether it was from his days as a student at St. Francis de Sales High School or his days at Columbia College, he was known as a gentle giant who stood about 6'3".

Arnold believed that he could make a difference in his community. Maybe it was his Roman Catholic upbringing that drove his altruistic nature. When our old church Saints Peter and Paul closed down, he became a regular at another South Chicago church called Our Lady of Guadalupe, located a little further West on 92nd Street. Arnold always believed that one person could make a difference, so he became very active with the Chicago Alternative Policing Strategy (CAPS). He would coordinate community meetings with the commander of Area 4, who was my fraternity brother and friend Fred Coffey. Fred was my sister Ramona's first commander when she joined CPD. One of our old neighbors from 90th and Jeffery, Connie Jordan, became a public defender for Cook County, and they would see each other in court from time to time.

Because Arnold worked closely with CAPS, he would meet my Alpha pledge son, Phillip Hampton, the director for the organization. Phillip married Dana White, the daughter of Hazel White, who grew up across the street from my dad in Nashville. Hazel also migrated to Chicago after graduating from Tennessee State University and became a long-time educator for Chicago Public Schools.

My dear friend Arnold would become a widely known beacon of hope in South Chicago. He would routinely take pictures of surrounding properties and report violations to city inspectors. As a result, he made some enemies! He was instrumental in the creation of a new law in Chicago specifically to levy heavy fines and arrest offending slum landlords. The first person in the city to be prosecuted under this law was because of Arnold's work. This landlord in particular did not like the light that this gentle soul decided to shine on the dark in the world!

"We can never go nowhere unless we share with each other." -
Tupac Shakur, "Changes"

"For now they kill me with a living death." - William Shakespeare,
Richard III

On December 29th, 1997, four days after Christmas and four months after I graduated from dental school, my phone rang with my sister Ramona on the other end. She sounded very upset. Then I heard "Mireles," and I KNEW it was NOT good news. There was a hazy sick feeling in my stomach. It was worse than that day my childhood sweetheart said she wanted a divorce. It was worse than any other disappointment or pain I had experienced. Did she say "dead"?

I remember my mind wandering and having scattered memories. I thought about Halloween because my friend was born on October 31st. I remembered trying to fix him up with this cute Mexican girl who worked with me at Marshall Field's at the State Street store. I remembered our goldenrod polo uniform shirts and brown uniform pants from Saints Peter and Paul. I remembered our confirmation by Bishop Hayes. I remember his old dog, a black terrier like my current dog Styxx. I remember that Kiss 45 he played in his parent's basement. Peter Criss was their drummer with the cat makeup.

Then I heard the words "YES, HE IS DEAD!" I cried! Arnold, one of the most nonviolent people I had ever known, was shot multiple times just steps from his home on Exchange Avenue. His red blood would stain the sidewalk a few blocks from our old grammar school.

In the Catholic Church, the color red symbolizes both Pentecost and the blood of Christ. The U.S. flag and the Mexican flag both have red in them. Red is a symbol of danger and also the color of the human heart! A person with the biggest of hearts bled for his community on December 29th, 1997.

He was gone and just like that, I was at a funeral!

My friend was murdered!

It was on TV!

It was in all the papers!

So unfair!

This was so much worse than getting divorced, because divorcing *had* to happen. This didn't have to happen. We couldn't be friends and brothers anymore. Arnold was gone!

Some lowlife hired killers for 10,000 pieces of silver! Goddamn Judas motherfucker! Over a damn fine! Just like that, Arnold was gone.

Arnold was a brother, a friend, an artist, a son, a world-changer, a lover of people, a Catholic and a kid from the South Side of Chicago. We had long since stopped being kids, but my life was made better because God made sure we became friends.

I was so proud to present his family with a Phoenix Award for Community Service from my chapter of Alpha, the Iota Delta Lambda Chapter. Phillip was representing Chicago Alternative Policing (CAPS) and the Mayor's Office to support Arnold, and he made the decision to join Alpha Phi Alpha at that event.

Arnold now has a street named after him in his beloved South Chicago. The public school across the street from our old grammar school, Phil Sheridan, was renamed "The Arnold Mireles Academy." This school is three blocks from that Victorian house he loved so much. There is a rendition of him on the school. Every time I look at it, I think, "Arnold would have done a better job." His fading picture makes me chuckle, but I still tear up a little when I look at it. I feel pride as I look at the mural featuring my old friend. He finally got his mural in South Chicago.

I have never understood why we have to experience pain, but I accept that WE MUST! I have tried to grasp why we must experience these events in our lives. Life is clearly about moving forward no matter what. Some people will start your life journey with you and finish with you, but many will not be there at the end.

The irony of life is that the most common thing for most of the people you meet in your life to do is to leave you at some point. Childhood friends move away, relatives die, you quit that job or you just lose touch. Sometimes you get divorced. Girlfriends and boyfriends break up. But even when bad things happen, life is mainly "Good Times." That ex-girlfriend taught you what you don't want in the next girlfriend. You learn to focus on the good times even after a failed relationship. That job you were fired from or quit was likely one that you hated anyway and probably didn't satisfy your true goal. There are many examples in our lives where we just have to hold on because there are more good times just around the corner.

I had to close my dental practice, much like when J.J. closed down his greeting card business. Closing my business made me very depressed, disappointed and ashamed. It wasn't as bad as my divorce or the death of my friend, but it taught me that there is always life after the storm and sometimes even better.

In my parents' house hangs my mother's picture of Jesus. That rendition of Jesus is the blond haired and blue-eyed image. No matter what I ever said to my mother, that is what Jesus looked like to her! Her point was that whatever He looked like, you needed to have faith in Him.

Mom always said that our life was truly about taking many great leaps of faith. James Evans initially thought that the Black Jesus painting was about luck, and he wanted to hold on to the picture as a good luck charm. But his wife, Florida, implored him to give the picture back to J.J. so he could enter it into an art contest. That TV mother also understood that it was all about faith.

You just have to believe that, regardless of what you are going through in life, "Bad Times" are usually balanced out with a greater number of "Good Times!"

"SCRATCHING AND SURVIVING."

*The Arnold Mireles Academy 9000 S. Exchange
Located across the Street from the former Saints Peter
and Paul School, South Chicago 60617*

169

Just lookin' out of the window

CHAPTER 21
After the Window Breaks

When I started writing this book four years ago, the plan was to present it to my parents in August of 2019 as a part of the celebration of the 20th anniversary of my marriage to Denise. Since my parents' anniversary is also in August, I hoped to recognize them for their 62nd anniversary as a part of the celebration. Their marriage was an inspiration to my sisters, and it was always important to me to recognize them.

Over the previous couple of years, my parents and I had spent a lot of time talking about family stories and history in anticipation of having people from both sides of my family present for our big day. Mom was my main collaborator who had a lifetime of report cards, certificates, newspaper articles, videos and pictures of the life she shared with her family.

I also started to realize that my parents were in their 80s and might not be around for many more of these celebrations, so I felt compelled to include something special for them during that party. Ironically, I still believed sometimes that they would be with me forever!

In 2017, my sisters, wife and I had a wonderful celebration for my parents' 60th wedding anniversary. We were so happy that so many friends and family helped us celebrate our parents' special day, I realized the need to maximize these moments before it was too late. My marathon running coach Mario Wiggins ironically taught me that simple concept. On a whim for my 40th birthday, I decided that I

171

wanted to run a marathon, and I would ultimately complete seven! I am a legacy runner for the Chicago Marathon. I have been blessed with a couple of new brothers-in-law in addition to my wife's brother Bob as my sisters found happiness. Two new nephews and a great-nephew were born.

It wasn't my dream when I joined the United States Army Reserves, but I ended up being deployed as a part of Operation Enduring Freedom after 9/11, which turned into a nightmare! I witnessed my favorite niece graduate from college as a nurse. Some of our friends got married and unfortunately divorced as well. Some of my childhood friends now have children in college, while some have obtained PhDs and other advanced degrees. My parents saw me open my dream dental practice, but that was one of my first adult dreams that I would have to give up when the economy went bad during the Great Recession of 2008.

My wife and I also experienced some tough losses of good friends like Dr. Charles Warnell and Dr. Ned Fleming, two of her Black medical partners. Though we have no children, euthanizing a couple of our beloved family pets was truly painful. Two of our dogs, Spanky and Smooches, had been with us from the beginning of our marriage and were an important part of our family. I would never compare pets to children, but those were tough losses!

The toughest loss was when my mother-in-law, Juanita Jackson, passed away in 2015 after a long illness. She was an integral part of my family. It was so hard when she passed away! My mother-in-love was one of our biggest cheerleaders, even when she became ill. She never let us forget how much we meant to her, and I will never forget what she meant to me. I promise that I will ALWAYS protect, love and honor your precious gift to me, Mrs. Juanita Jackson! And I will look out for my great brother-in-law, your son Robert Jackson Jr.!

In spite of these challenges, my bride of more than 20 years has been with me every step of the way. Because of faith and her love, every moment has been bearable. My wife Denise is so much like my mother. I think my mother has always loved her because of the kind spirit they both share. They loved each other and they both love me, which has been one of my greatest rewards. Each of these women knows me as well as I know myself. I draw strength from their presence like Superman does from the radiant sun. It gave me great joy to watch my mother fall in love with my wife.

2019 was to be a major milestone for us. I was so excited about planning to celebrate my 20 years of marriage with my wife. I wanted to be like my parents who had been married so long. My first marriage didn't last that long, relatively speaking, so I sometimes wondered if I was cut out to be a husband. Would anyone stick by like my mom did with my father? My nearly 22-year marriage has dispelled those doubts!

We had the best of plans for this monumental year. But in January of that year, Dad called me and asked me to come over because he needed to talk to me, and that was when my world changed forever! This call came a few weeks after we celebrated his 83rd birthday on January 1st, 2019.

When Denise and I arrived at my parents' house, it just seemed different. Once the hugs were complete, I noticed the odd look on my mother's face as she was seated at the kitchen table. I could tell that something was on her mind. Once we sat down, Dad's voice started to crack as he told us, "Your mother has colon cancer."

"That couldn't be" was my initial thought, until I remembered that Mom's sister Mildred had that same condition and died from it. Colon cancer runs in the Owens family. My uncle Moses and aunt Esther are colon cancer survivors. Mom was the fourth of her 13 siblings to be afflicted with the condition, and she was turning 83 on March 27th. No way this was happening now, since we just celebrated Christmas and Dad's birthday! This can't be right!

I thought I must have heard it wrong, but when I saw the tears flowing down my mother's cheeks, I knew. I wanted to be strong. "Don't cry," I said to myself, but I started to cry. We had been there 10 years earlier with Dad when he told us that he had prostate cancer at that same table. I began to hate that damn table! But Dad was a 10-year survivor.

Dad wanted Denise and me to go with them to the next doctor's appointment to discuss options. I had married a doctor, so in my head, I was like "we got this!" while having "WHAT THE FUCK!" emotions after we left my parents' house in disbelief.

Before we left, Mom was saying things like "This is in Jesus' hands," and then I saw the White image of Jesus that hangs over Dad's favorite chair. Each day, he and Mom sat in adjacent chairs watching television in that living room, and there was White Jesus above the same spot where Dad sits.

Denise and I went to that doctor's appointment with my parents, and the plan of man was laid out, so surgery it was going to be. One of the surgeons was a Haitian brother who spoke with a thick accent. My mother joked about knowing how to understand him from working with her good friend Marie Noisette in the instruments department at Mercy Hospital. He was the main surgeon, but his schedule was full, so he introduced us to a very nice female Hispanic doctor who was going to do the procedure. My sister Vanessa had that emergency colostomy years ago when she was in grammar school, and what the doctors described sounded very similar to that surgery.

On the day of the surgery, Mom's husband, her firstborn son, her two daughters, our spouses and her only granddaughter gathered at the hospital. We were worried and scared as she went to surgery, but confident. After a few hours, Mom was in the recovery room and the surgeon said, "We think we got it all!"

Days later, Mom's labs were great, and the pathology report said no cancer on either portion of the colon. Thank God! After a short hospital stay, Mom went home, though her colon was in two pieces just like when Vanessa came home from her surgery. About a month later, the surgeons resected her colon and put her on prophylactic chemotherapy as a precaution. All seemed cool!

A few months later in March, we were gathered as a family over my parents' house for Mom's 83rd birthday, but I noticed that Mom had lost a lot of weight. Dad was complaining to me saying, "Your mom doesn't like anything that I cook for her," which was weird because Dad is a great cook and she ate everything he made.

The birthday was a potluck, so I called and asked my mother what she wanted me to bring. She replied, "Some catfish from the Dixie Kitchen." The Dixie Kitchen was the same restaurant that Denise and I went to on our first date, but it was now located in Lansing, about 10 minutes from my parents' home in Lynwood. If my mother wanted catfish, she was getting her catfish!

At the celebration, we also had cakes and other treats that Dad had prepared and some that my sister had bought. I watched Mom with that catfish and noticed that she didn't really eat. She was humoring me, but she barely touched it. At the dinner, we had our usual family banter and ribbing, but Mom was so tired!

Out of the blue, Mom asked me to go downstairs to the basement where her other television was and get all of the VHS tapes stored under it and take them to get them converted to DVD. My sisters had been converting my mother's many photo albums into DVDs for a few years, so it wasn't totally strange, but why now?

The basement television cabinet was where the various Super 8 movies and video recordings of family reunions, graduations and birthday parties, which were her prized family memories, were kept. Mom was so insistent on that day that I take them ALL! Being the dutiful son who was little annoyed, I said, "Okay, Mom!" I packed them up in a shopping bag and took them home.

Mom would so proudly show guests those tapes, which included things like my graduation from dental school and my nephew Andrae's birthday party when we rented a pony for him when he was about six years old. There were family reunions and trips to Nashville on those VHS tapes, too.

There were a lifetime of memories in that cabinet. There was a flood a couple of years back that destroyed some pictures, and Mom wanted those memories protected. The only pictures of our pet ducks were destroyed in that flood.

Before we left, my dad and I had one of our side conversations while Denise was chatting as always with my mother. Dad insisted that something was not right and said, "YOU need to check on your mother more!" I was a little pissed, but accepted what my dad said. He always gives it to you raw, but he is always right. On the way home, Denise and I were both distracted. I followed Dad's instructions by calling and visiting Mom more, but noticed she was smiling less and just so tired.

On Mother's Day, we were once again over my parents' home, and I had something very special for Mom that I thought would cheer her up. It was a draft of THIS book. She had been helping with it, and I was so excited about showing it to her. I had printed off the pages of the book that I had been working on for a couple of years.

Before I completed it, Mom had recently given me details about some other things from my childhood that I couldn't remember. She also told me things about her family that she had never shared before, like about having a half-brother. Mom had been recalling all kind of stories. She even asked my sister Vanessa to take her to the old house on Jeffery because she wanted to visit old neighbors like the Hoseas who were still living there. She also went to visit her old friend Mrs. Fields, who couldn't see her because she was too ill.

My book was about my life with the family she helped to create. I just needed to give it to her! I worked day and night for a couple of weeks before I put it in a binder and signed it from her son. I just had to do it. I DON'T KNOW WHY. When I gave it to my mother, I asked her to read it, and I noticed that she had lost more weight!

Before Denise and I left for home, Mom asked me to get ALL of her gospel records and take them home because her record player was broken. This didn't make sense because she hadn't had a turntable in years, so I thought it was a strange request. But I gathered the records and took them home. Some of those records were from Antioch Church and featured Reverend Daniels, her first minister when she and Dad arrived in Nashville. Mom was very protective of these old vinyl albums, and it was really odd that she wanted me to have them.

Mother's Day was on Sunday, and my birthday was several days later as it always had been, since I was born in May of 1963. When the 15th of May came and went without Mom calling me, it started becoming clearer that something was wrong. I was her firstborn and her favorite in my mind, but Mom's spirit was in another place!

My mother made everyone she ever met feel like they were her favorite. I have been sharing MY mother with everyone else in the world, but when I saw her the next weekend, I never mentioned to her that my feelings were hurt. Something was not right!

The Thursday before Labor Day, Dad calls and says, "I am with your mom at Community Hospital." Oh shit! Denise and I are there in an hour. When we arrive, Mom is on a stretcher in the hallway waiting to go into an exam room. The night before, Mom had gone to sleep on the basement floor because she had fallen and was too weak to get up. My dad woke up that morning and realized that she hadn't come to bed. When he went to the basement, he found her on the floor curled up and was beside himself.

Mom said she didn't want to bother him, so she hadn't called him for help, which angered him. Dad called my sister Vanessa, who lived five minutes away, to help get Mom off the floor, and they put her into the car to take her to her doctor.

Once Mom's primary care physician saw her, she decided that Mom was so sick that she called 911 for an ambulance. Mom was transported to Community Hospital in Munster, Indiana, because her regular hospital, St. Margaret Mercy in Dyer, Indiana, was on bypass. When Denise completed her family medicine residency at Cook County Hospital, her first job was at Hammond Clinic, which required her to be on staff at both Community and St. Margaret Mercy. I knew Mom really wanted to be at her regular hospital, St. Margaret Mercy, because she hated Community Hospital!

Denise and I were able to hang out with Mom in an exam room while waiting for her to be transferred to a room on the floor. We actually were having a little fun in that exam room while giggling at the All in the Family and The Jeffersons reboot episodes that were on

177

television. Jamie Foxx was hilarious! It was great to see Marla Gibbs reprise her role as Florence as well.

Those were two of those Norman Lear shows like Good Times that my family watched many years ago. Mom was actually acting like her old self, so I wasn't worried. We were joking, and Mom was cracking on me as only a mother could do, asking Denise how much I had gotten on her nerves lately.

They sent her upstairs to one of the nicest hospital rooms I had ever seen. When I left Mom that night, I was not worried because she was smiling. She had not been smiling lately, and it was a good thing to see, even in a hospital room. She was even telling some more of her silly jokes, so it was going to be all right.

Because it was Memorial Day weekend, an on-call doctor checked on my mom. She described pain in the area of her cancer surgery, so he planned to scan her belly. Though her colon had been resected, she still hadn't really been eating solid food. Mom kept saying her food "don't taste like anything." The doctor suspected an infection near her surgical site, so I hung out with Mom and left when visiting hours were over.

The next day, Mom was a little loopy, but she had the scan. The doctor said that he saw something in the area of her surgery. He wanted to go in with a scope to check it out, but he said that with it being the holiday weekend, assembling a surgical team was going to be challenging, so he wanted to put that off until after the holiday had passed.

Mom ended up staying though the weekend, but by Saturday, she started struggling with her memory. She also seemed not to be able to get comfortable and kept asking for pillows and to be moved in and out of bed. She was talking, but seemed to be confusing things.

The on-call doctor decided that surgery was going to wait so it could be done at Mom's regular hospital, St. Margaret Mercy, about 15 minutes from their Lynwood home. That weekend was just terrible because Mom began acting more and more erratic. Finally, on Tuesday, she was transferred. That exploratory surgery was now going to happen Thursday morning with her regular team in the comfort of a faith-based hospital, which was reassuring. That gave us comfort!

On Wednesday night, I was working late until 7 p.m. and received a text about Mom being moved to the ICU at the hospital. When I read the text, I thought my sister was telling me that visiting hours ended at 8 p.m., which meant I couldn't make it there from my job in Frankfort. She was actually trying to tell me that the second set of visiting hours started at 8 p.m.

Because of the confusion, I decided to go to a Brotherhood toast in honor of my fraternity brother Eddie Jones, who had passed away a couple of days before. I knew that I was unlikely to be able to attend his upcoming funeral on Saturday, so I decided to support him by attending the toast for a few hours. Eddie was my Chapter President and one of the first people I saw when I was initiated in the early hours on a summer day in August of 1987. When my wife Denise had a surprise 40th birthday party, it was Eddie who got me there.

The event for Eddie occurred at what we call the "Alpha House" on 83rd and Western, known as the XL Center. I went after work at 7:30 p.m. Eddie invited me for years to attend the Alpha Fellowship night on Wednesdays at that facility, but I worked late on Wednesdays and never went. I decided that I would go just this one time. When I arrived, I saw scores of brothers that I had not seen in years, because Eddie was very popular.

I was distracted from what was going on with my mom and having a good time until another member came over to me with his cell phone. Linwood Wallace, my pledge father, was on the phone. This was weird because I saw him leave earlier. He told me, "Denise has been trying to call you for an hour." When I looked at my own phone, I realized that it was dead, and my heart sank! She never calls me in a situation like that unless it is an emergency.

I thanked Linwood for getting me the message and hopped in my car and plugged my phone in the charger. It took a few minutes to get enough charge to make a call. When I finally got a two percent charge,

I reached Denise, who answered sounding obviously upset and asked, "Where are you?"

I was screaming at her that my phone was dead when she tried to call me. She said she had been calling for hours and called three frat brothers trying to find me. Dad had also been calling and was very upset that he could not reach me. When I called him back, he said, "You need to get to the hospital now," and then hung up!

Denise was probably concerned about my state of mind, so she called me back and said she could meet me at the house so we could go together. Once I arrived at our home, Denise hopped into my car and we sped to Dyer, Indiana. Once at the hospital, we signed in through the ER because it was after midnight and went upstairs to the ICU. When we went into the room, Mom was flailing in the bed and moaning. When I saw my mother, I screamed, "Mom, do you know who this is?" and she moaned, "Keith!" which gave me momentary comfort.

I called my dad, who had gone home. He was really angry at me. He asked where I had been, since he was trying to call me. I was really upset and began crying and tried to defend my actions. My dad just said the surgery was scheduled for 7 a.m. the next morning and that we all needed to be there. We sat with my mom for an hour, then went home to get some rest for the morning.

I don't think I slept that night at all. I got up and left the next morning without eating. I arrived at the hospital at 7:15 a.m. Dad was already in the ICU with Mom, my sister Vanessa and my niece Alyssa. Ramona was in the waiting area waiting for me. The attending surgeon then gathered us all in the waiting area while they prepped Mom for surgery.

She told us the plan was that the anesthesia department would come down and intubate her, and then she would go to surgery and see what was what. Mom's breathing was so bad that she had been intubated before the surgeon even arrived. Oh hell!

We all then went into that ICU, and my dad kissed his wife. The rest of us kissed our mother and grandmother as she was wheeled off. We went back to the waiting room with good thoughts until ten minutes later when the same surgeon came in the room and said, "Your mother is too unstable for us to do the procedure on her now."

Well, hell, if not now, when? Mom was wheeled back into the ICU. Only three people could be in the room with her at a time, so we took shifts going into see Mom, who had monitors and oxygen running. The respirator was clicking as it went up and down. It was surreal!

After a couple of hours, Mom's kidneys stopped working, so they put her on dialysis. After about an hour into dialysis, the doctor said, "She is clotting, so we have to stop dialysis." At this point, Mom was not really breathing on her own, and her kidneys weren't working. Why did I have to remember my human physiology class?

For the next couple of hours, we were in and out of the rooms, rotating from the ICU to the waiting room. We all were just really quiet. The beeps on the machines which warn that a bodily function is underperforming were going off a lot now. This is a nightmare... WAKE UP!

My sister put in a call to Andrae, her oldest son, to come to the hospital right away! I didn't know what to do, so I called my pastor, Fr. Andrew Smith, and told him that we needed him. He traveled to Northwest Indiana from our Bronzeville church. When he arrived, he simply asked me, "What do you need?" Then he asked, "Do you want me to do her last rites?" I didn't want to claim that, so I just asked him to pray with my family. We prayed together, held hands and cried. We prayed, but I didn't feel any better afterwards. I thanked my brother Fr. Drew for his support.

It meant much in that moment, but that prayer felt like a fantasy. Please, Mom, don't go! Then I looked at my mother and said another prayer, "Please, God, take my mother!" I didn't want my mother to leave, but she was suffering now. I love my mother! I wanted to tell her I loved her! I hope she knows that I love her! I hope I made her proud! Please, GOD, tell her I did my best! This day sucks so bad. Her blood pressure is now 42 over 16. Respirations 12. I hate this shit!

There was a short time after Fr. Drew left when it was just Dad and me. Dad was just staring at my mother, his wife, and I told him, "You were the best husband ever to my mother. She loved you very much, Dad! You know that, right?" I told him that I knew that he loved her very much! I also thanked him for picking the best mother a person could ever have. He said "thank you" and wiped away some tears.

We were all gathered back in that room. My brother-in-law Gregory, who hates hospitals, was there most of the day with my wife, my two sisters, my niece and Dad. My sister Ramona put her phone to Mom's ear and played Mahalia Jackson singing "Precious Lord," which is her favorite song.

Ramona's husband, my nephew Andrae and his lady Liya were there by now. Andrae went to his grandmother's side and said some things to her and kissed her. My mother was so proud of the young man he grew up to be. I was watching him and the machines above my mother when about 10 minutes later, I saw IT! Dad said, "Your mother is snoring!" But my wife Denise (a doctor), my niece Alyssa (a registered nurse), my sister Ramona (a Chicago Police Officer), my sister Vanessa (an occupational therapist) and I (a dentist) cringed at that sound! We KNEW that was not snoring! Maybe if we don't say it, it won't be true. If we wake up, this will just have been a bad dream.

In that moment, a doctor walked in the room and said, "I need the room." I looked at this dude like he was crazy, and we filed out the door past this inconsiderate bastard. Five minutes later, he came out of my mother's room to where we were standing at the nurse's station and mumbled some shit, then said, "I am sorry for your loss," and walked the hell into the sunset.

We then went into that room, where the tube was now out of her mouth. We were so sad and crying until my dad looked down at his wife, my beautiful mother, and said, "Look, she is smiling!" For the first time in many months, I saw her! There she was, my mother! She WAS smiling and at peace. She waited for her grandson and knew her job as faithful servant was done! She was in God's house now!

I was too mad and hurt to appreciate it, and I proceeded to demand that the doctor who just left come back and make this right! I was cursing and screaming in this Catholic hospital and started to question if these people (men and women) had done EVERYTHING they could to save my mother. What was he going to do to really make this right? That was pure emotion screaming out.

It was in that moment that I got it. I have always had to learn stuff the hard way. I always have to go down the wrong street first, and this was no different. Mom always said if you have done your best, then all would be taken care of by God.

My wife later let me in on the conversation she had with my mother on Mother's Day. Mom told her that she had seen Jesus and that everything was going to be all right. She also said that loving, accepting and forgiving people is the most important thing to do.

Every time in my life when I felt like I was a failure or was scared to go to a school where people hated me, my mom walked with me, whether literally or spiritually. On that first day at Joseph Warren School, she reminded me that someday I would have to leave home without her. With my mother, it didn't matter if others thought that I was not smart enough, rich enough, fast enough or any other reason to belong somewhere, because she told me that l did belong!

She gave me some of the most important gifts that money can't buy, which are faith and love. My mother ALWAYS had faith in God, and she ALWAYS had faith in her family, who she LOVED until her last breath. Mom believed in God and that love was God. Faith is the thread that ties love and God together. It was hard to let my mother go, but she had gone home. She is our angel now. She had been trying to tell us for a while.

The night before we held my mother's visitation, my sister Vanessa had a gun pulled out on her as she was walking into our father's house. We never experienced anything like that in 32 years of my parents living in that house. Her daughter Alyssa and my father had no clue what was happening on the porch just outside, where they were seated.

A gunman had put a gun to my sister's temple and said, "Don't turn around, and give me the keys!"

She took the keys that were in one hand and passed them backwards. In her other hand was a tiny bag with a rosary that my good friend Rosemary Sykes had given to me to use at my mother's funeral. It had a picture of Mary, the mother of Jesus, on it. The gunman took the keys, started the car and screeched off without harming my sister. Our Mother in Heaven protected her daughter that day! I truly believe that rosary symbolized my mother standing with Mary in heaven.

My mother spent 56 years showing me life through a window that was held in place and framed by faith and love. That window could be found anywhere YOU call home, whether it be the projects or a palace. Home is what YOU make of it. Living in the projects or in a country farmhouse does not define you. Mom consistently told me that there are NO limits to what you can be if you have faith.

You can't ever be afraid to fail. To fail is not to try!

Mom saw things in me even when I didn't. She used to make me speak at family gatherings, which would drive me crazy, but my mother wanted me to use my voice and tell my story.

My mother also helped me find my faith by putting me into Catholic school, which is where I met another of my angels, Arnold Mireles. My running coach, Mr. Mario Wiggins, is an educator who had his very first teaching job at the Arnold Mireles Academy. That coach gave me what I will call a message from my friend Arnold when he shared his personal mantra to "maximize the moments!"

When I was calling my mother's friends to give them the details about Mom's funeral, I was told a story by her friend and former co-worker Marie Noisette. When Mom worked at Mercy, she started in housekeeping when an opportunity presented itself to work for higher pay in the department that sterilized surgical instruments.

Mom was not college educated and knew nothing about the hundreds of surgical instruments used in the various procedures, but she became one of the first Black people to work in the department.

She worked her butt off to learn all of those instruments! Surgeons notoriously go crazy when trays are incorrect during a procedure, but Mom mastered them, so the doctors at Mercy loved her!

While Mom worked in the department, there were other Black workers who were Haitian immigrants, including Marie. She and these immigrants were drawn to the department for the pay as well as for an opportunity to put down their mops and brooms. These non-college-educated women soon dominated the department.

In the late '70s, an initiative was imposed by the hospital when a new White manager decided that all instrument technicians needed to be certified by a local college in order to work in the department. Obviously, Mom and the other Blacks in the department did not have this certification.

Mom recognized the ploy as an attempt to fire the mainly Black staff, most of whom were wives who worked to support their families. When this new White manager held a meeting to implement the new plan, the Black workers were very fearful and certainly thought they were going to be fired. My mom knew what was going on and decided to stand up and ask the White guy, "Why are you changing the rules on us?"

The White guy really didn't appreciate being challenged by this uneducated Black woman and responded by telling my mother that she could go to school downtown, take classes at the school and get certified after taking a test. These women didn't have any extra time or money for some expensive school, so Mom cut to the chase and asked, "What if we take and pass the test? Can we keep our jobs?" The incredulous White guy couldn't believe the question, or that this Black woman with no college education or formal training dared to ask, and said "sure."

He definitely did not know Alease "Eechie" Owens Wilson of Fayetteville, Tennessee. She didn't have a college degree, but she was a very smart woman. Her older sister Lorraine (Rene) at 17 raised her and her younger siblings when their dad passed away. Rene was not above putting a switch to her baby sister's backside when she messed up on her lessons. This same older sister, a high school dropout, raised five children who are now all graduates of Tennessee State University. Mom was not an educated teacher but was a TEACHER, just like her big sister. Alease Wilson raised kids who would attend Catholic grammar and high school, and we all attended college.

My Mom hatched a plan where this lady from Fayetteville with no training would hold classes at lunchtime. She tutored each pupil on the various instruments and their purpose. Dad and her Haitian friends made dishes for these "lunch and learn" sessions held in the cafeteria. They also went over each other's homes and practiced and memorized what Professor Wilson was teaching them. When the test was given, ALL OF THEM PASSED IT!

Now, Dr. Keith P. Wilson gets to tell HER story.

Mom saw HER daughter put on a police uniform for the Chicago Police Department and HER daughter became an occupational therapist. Mom loved her husband who loved her back for nearly 62 years. Mom saw her grandchildren succeed too! Granddaughter Alyssa became a registered nurse, and Mom's grandsons become respectable young men. She saw all three of her children happily married and even has a great-grandchild.

Mom showed me all of these things through her window for 56 years and two weeks of my life. That window broke a few weeks ago when she went to heaven, but I have learned enough to replace it with my own.

My mother knew how to love, and she loved her family. I know that love is God, but I still miss my mother. Dad knew a good thing when he saw it, which is why he married my mother so soon after coming back from the military and moved with an urgency to start a new life with her. Dad and Mom were absolutely evenly yoked!

As I think about my mom going to sleep for the last time with her whole family around her, it was like old times when we all were in that little house on Jeffery. We were physically and emotionally close. Like the last moments on The Waltons when everyone said "Good night, John Boy," we were just happy and content that we were all together.

Mom knew that her family was still together when she went to be with God.

Mom could take her rest knowing that her family had done great things together. She knew that we kids would look out for each other and the love of her life, Dad. Her kids knew to work hard but remain humble.

Mom had been that faithful servant and would be celebrated in heaven for a job well done. She had taught us to just do the right thing and to not look for a reward or thanks, because doing the right thing was the reward.

Sometimes you will have to endure hurt and just need to learn to heal from it. Forgive always, but never forget, as that would be foolish.

Degrees, money, fancy homes and cars will come and go, but the true riches of faith and love can't be taken away.

On May 30th, 2019, I saw Mom smile for her family as they took that tube out of her mouth, though her soul had already taken flight towards heaven.

My mom was dreaming and flying for real.

Her firstborn knew what he had to do, and that was to continue her dream and never give up!

I will keep dreaming!

I love you, Mom!

-Keith

"Life is lived before a live studio audience!"

Cue Earth, Wind & Fire's "That's the Way of The World"

Fade to Black

Just lookin' out of the window

AFTERWORD

By Fr Andrew Charles Smith, Pastor of
Holy Angels Catholic Church of Chicago

Dr. Keith Wilson's memoirs reflect a life centered upon God, family, and the tough but nurturing streets of Chicago. He uses the famed television show Good Times as a background for his upbringing. Good Times featured a close-knit African American family guided by the presence and strength of an African American father.

Dr. Wilson was blessed to be raised in the similar nucleus of a loving family. He speaks of his mother's wisdom, love, and guidance as he journeyed to manhood. Moreover, he speaks of his Roman Catholic faith and education as the keys to his success.

Dr. Wilson persevered in his studies and became a dentist and a positive role model for young African American men. He is an active member of Alpha Phi Alpha fraternity, a strong African American fraternity that continues to provide community service programs for the African American community.

Furthermore, Dr. Wilson highlights Chicago's African American culture, including the many African American artists who were born in Chicago and contributed to its rich cultural heritage. For example, the Bronzeville neighborhood is known for its 20th-century African American residents, who included Louis Armstrong and Gwendolyn Brooks, and the annual Bud Billiken Parade.

Dr. Wilson's book is an enjoyable read. It shows the importance and beauty of family life. In addition, it brings back memories of a time when life was sweet despite the challenges many African Americans faced growing up on the South Side of Chicago.

Just lookin' out of the window

197

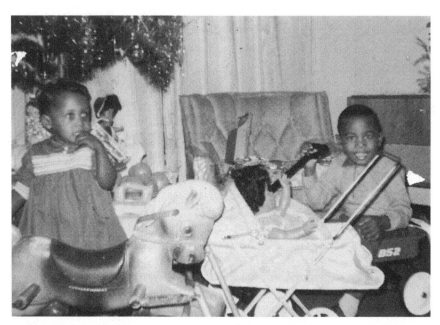

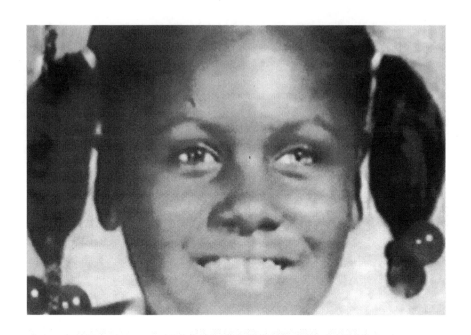

221

Just lookin' out of the window

Made in United States
Orlando, FL
12 August 2022

20929894R00133